CONSUMING YOUTH

LEADING TEENS THROUGH CONSUMER CULTURE

D1365158

John Berard • James Penner • Rick Bartlett

CONSUMING YOUTH

YOUTH

LEADING
TEENS
THROUGH
CONSUMER
CULTURE

John Berard · James Penner · Rick Bartlett

YOUTH
SPECIALTIES

ACADEMIC

ZONDERVAN.com/
AUTHORTRACKER
follow your favorite authors

ZONDERVAN

Consuming Youth
Copyright © 2010 by John Berard, James Penner, and Rick Bartlett

YS Youth Specialties is a trademark of YOUTHWORKS!, INCORPORATED and is registered with the United States Patent and Trademark Office.

This title is also available as a Zondervan ebook. Visit www.zondervan.com/ebooks.

Requests for information should be addressed to:

Zondervan, Grand Rapids, Michigan 49530

Library of Congress Cataloging-in-Publication Data

Berard, John.
　　Consuming youth / John Berard, Rick Bartlett, and James Penner.
　　　　p.　cm.
　　Includes bibliographical references (p.　　　).
　　ISBN　978-0-310-66935-7
　　　1. Church work with teenagers.　2. Church work with youth.　I. Bartlett, Rick.
　II. Penner, James (James Allan) III. Title.
　BV4447.B475 2010
　259'.23—dc22　　　　　　　　　　　　　　　　　　　　　　　　　2010037697

Cover design: Anderson Design Group
Interior design: David Conn

Printed in the United States of America

10　11　12　13　14　/DCI/　20　19　18　17　16　15　14　13　12　11　10　9　8　7　6　5　4　3　2　1

Bethany, Leah, Julianne,
Elya, Erick,
Grace, and Toby
... our kids, who bring immense joy
and teach us the importance of
vocation every day.

CONTENTS

ACKNOWLEDGMENTS

We'd like to thank the following people and organizations for all of the important reasons . . . and for their support of this writing project.

From John: To the one who supports me beyond reason and encourages me continually—my wife, Kathy. This book wouldn't have made it out the door without you, and saying thank you doesn't come close to expressing my appreciation for the many ways in which you make things possible. Even so . . . thank you. And to our kids, who always asked me how it was going, thank you. No father could be more proud of who you are and who you're becoming than me. There is no greater joy than that of being with you as you grow up. Thank you to the YFC national training staff for your encouragement and for enduring my busyness now and then while I was completing this project. Your dedication to your work makes our work together far better. To the colleagues within YFC (you know who you are)—encouragers all—thanks for always asking. Thanks to Jamie at st. benedict's table for freeing up space when I needed it and the encouragement . . . I'm very grateful for the community. Thank you to Wayne Tomalty—a colleague, youth worker, teacher, and longtime friend—for carefully reading and offering useful feedback and suggestions. To our YFC partners, friends all and many of you have been in our corner from the beginning . . . even long before the YFC days—that, well, is simply astonishing. Thank you.

From James: To Claire, who continues to be my best friend on earth and was there throughout this adventure. To Elya and Erick, who keep making me proud by their solid decisions. To Claire's and my inspirational parents, who keep fusing adult faith and childlike passion. I want to be like you in old age! To the InterVarsity Christian Fellowship community who nurtured me this past quarter-century and then freed me up to be a full-time youth sociologist and consultant. To many University of Lethbridge faculty and students who keep shaping me as a sociologist, educator, and—best of all—friend. To countless friends, family, research assistants—all encouragers—you know who you are. To my five mentor friends- Reg Bibby, Jeff Carter, Loretta Gillis, Peter Hanhart, and Patrick Lenon- who have blessed me with their wisdom and constant support. For Loretta, Rosalie, Isabel, and Jean—the sisters of Saint Martha—for Room 2 at the retreat center throughout the writing process. To God—you fill me with joy and leave me speechless . . . and listening.

From Rick: I'd like to thank the staff of Ministry Quest: Cam, Anne, Mike, Rhonda, and John, who've modeled these principles and traveled with me on this journey. Thanks to the more than 200 high school participants and churches who've put into practice the principles expressed here. Thank you to the staff, faculty, and students at MB Biblical Seminary in Fresno, Langley, and Winnipeg, for conversations in classes and during lunches when I was able to think about the ideas and concepts presented in this book. Thanks to Leonard Sweet and the LEC2 cohort at George Fox Seminary's D.Min. program—Leadership in the Emerging Culture. These concepts came alive through my conversations, writing, and online interactions with you as my brothers on this journey. To my "preteens," Grace and Toby, who keep me thinking and living with youth in mind. May you both grow up to be kids who are "ruined for normal." Most of all, thanks to my wife, Karen, a strong supporter, an encourager, and a partner in ministry. This wouldn't have come about without your help.

From John, James, and Rick: We are deeply grateful to Youth Specialties and Zondervan for undertaking this project, and we're appreciative of Jay Howver's commitment. Thank you, Jay, for giving the nod and life to this idea and to Roni Meek for graciously and patiently leading the book to completion. Thanks to Dave Urbanski for skillfully guiding us and taking the book to a much better place than it was when he got it. And thanks to Laura Gross for her keen eye throughout. And to the rest of their team who had a hand in this project—thank you. A journey you all have made more than worthwhile.

INTRODUCTION

Growing Up Cool:
The Business of Cool Hunters

*Who decides what's cool? Certain kids in certain places—
and only the cool hunters know who they are.*

—Malcolm Gladwell[1]

*Kids are being marketed to from the moment they're born.
And they're not just being marketed products, they're being
marketed values . . . And the values are: "Things can make
me cool; things define my self-worth."*

—Susan Linn[2]

On one particular day, while walking through the mall on our way to grab a coffee, my teenage companion's cell phone beeped with a text message. He unquestioningly read the message as we passed the DVD store windows where huge posters called to our attention the newest releases. I think Pavlov would be pleased with the savvy of the makers of all things techie that now rule the marketplace. And the reason for the text message interruption—maybe it was a message from a friend or relative? Not this one—it was an ad targeted directly to my young friend.

In a very crowded commercial world, advertisers are feeling the squeeze. Marketers have to narrowcast their advertising. It's like that scene from *Minority Report* in which John Anderton (Tom Cruise) is on the run in a futuristic mall while sporting a new pair of eyeballs in an attempt to avoid detection by the advanced technology that scans and locates people. As John glances at the video billboards he passes, they register the scan of his newly implanted eyes and begin advertising directly to him by name, complete with references to the latest purchase.

We aren't there yet, but corporations can interrupt our days and our space at any time: the text message about the hot stock tip; the email about that special "getaway" contest sponsored by the local newspaper and the airline; the phone call from the bank about a fraud protection service; the YouTube comedy clip that was actually a car commercial; the offer in the mail for a new credit card, as well as the red-letter alert offering a free mystery gift for renewing a magazine subscription—now! What do we do with what seems to be an all-out assault for not only our money, but also, ultimately, our loyalty?

Now imagine you're thirteen years old. You feel unsure of yourself and your place in the world, yet you're living in the midst of a daily blizzard of ads and brands that are all focused on getting your attention, your money, and your fidelity.

On any given day, a savvy new breed of researchers might be sorting through stacks of market data. They might be creating surveys or hosting focus groups. They might be roaming the streets, walking the malls, or visiting schools and even homes. What are they after? In the simplest terms: teenagers. But to get them, they first must find the next big thing—that thing for which teenagers will be more than willing to put their cash on the counter. "They" are the cool hunters—creators and sellers of popular culture. Their business is selling to teenagers, a red-hot consumer demographic worth billions of dollars. They are the merchants of cool.[3]

Cool hunters not only find and define "cool," but they also create and cooperate with marketers and companies to build a branded culture in which logos and brands take on a personality, a lifestyle, an image, and a set of values. Journalist Alissa Quart chronicles the branding of teenagers in her book *Branded: The Buying and Selling of Teenagers* and relates how one corporate marketer made the claim that "the average ten-year-old boy has memorized from three hundred to four hundred brands. Ninety-two percent of kids request brand-specific products."[4] Branding is just one aspect of the conditioning effects that a consumer culture offers teenagers. Image, desire, tastes, leisure, values, and vocation are but a few of the things profoundly shaped by the effects of a consumer culture.

The Business of Selling Cool

On one particular day, the consumer affairs program *Marketplace*, on CBC television, broadcasts "Buying into Sexy: The Sexing Up of Tweens." It's a report on how marketers are selling a grown-up, sexy image to preteen girls.[5] On the same program, they also check in with preteen guys to find out what they think about girls dressing sexy. What do they find? They discover that the "midriff" and the "mook," carefully constructed creations of the merchants of cool, are finding a home. Picture Mary Shelley's monster in *Frankenstein*: the scientist Victor Frankenstein learns to create a life that looks like a man but is, in fact, a much larger, much more powerful creation. The midriff and the mook—marketing images created by marketers for marketers—have become larger-than-life creations that now effectively shape the world of teenagers. But are marketers simply reflecting teens' desires, or have they begun to manufacture those desires in an attempt to capture the billions of dollars that are available from the teen market? And have they gone too far in their attempts to reach the hearts, minds, and wallets of teenagers?

On any given day, teenagers face decisions fueled by unlimited and unfiltered information. Some decisions are benign, while others carry with them a lifetime of possibilities. It seems that nowadays growing up is harder to do, with a complexity that runs deeper than the worn-out cultural expression: "Sex, drugs, and rock 'n' roll."

"The images and stories that bombard young people nowadays are many-faceted and ambiguous and enticing. The hustle and bustle is so fast, so pervasive. The stimulation from all our media is so overwhelming. The storing mechanisms and the space to interrogate yourself, and to be closely related to others you can trust—these are all now harder to find."[6] The story, the space, and the connection, when taken together, function as a means of shaping and informing the transitional period from youth to adulthood. And as James Fowler indicates, they're not only harder to find but also must now be understood within the context of a corporately driven, capitalistic agenda. The relentless formation of consumer culture powerfully shapes the story of what it means to grow up—what it means to become adult. This script, youth are told, offers meaning and purpose. But, does it?

The Contours of This Book

On one particular day, two friends were downcast and disoriented as they walked home with the news about losing a friend. Along the way a stranger asked what had them in such a discouraged state of mind. In disbelief, they asked the stranger how he couldn't know what had happened. And with that, the stranger walked and talked with these two friends, taking them through a history lesson of sorts that started with their questions and ended with the sharing of a meal. At that moment the two friends finally "saw" who they'd just spent the day with. In that instant they felt the familiar presence of their friend deep in their bones and burning in their hearts.[7]

The story of the disciples on the road to Emmaus reminds us of relationship as it speaks about the ordinary and also something familiar. There is a familiarity about the despair and disbelief in the hearts and minds of the disciples that resembles the myriad engaged youth workers who tirelessly work with teenagers and young adults today. And there is a certain level of despair and disbelief among youth and young adults as well. This isn't to say that all young people are walking around with their heads in their hands—far from it. In fact many young people are thriving.

But as William Damon—professor of education at Stanford University—writes in his new study, *The Path to Purpose*, "Others only appear to be doing well, and far too many seem stuck, rudderless and lacking a sense of what they want to do with their lives."[8] Even the casual observer of youth culture can notice a general and growing angst among them. It's become more ubiquitous in their movies, their music, their magazines, their novels—and it's showing up in their survey responses. It's also in their lives. Thus, both teenagers and those who spend time with them are left to wonder where Jesus is in the mix and what, if anything, his presence means to them and their social world.

The road to Emmaus story also tells of the very ordinary way in which the disciples met Jesus. In the midst of doing what they were doing, he was there. In the ordinary space there was conversation, and in the regular details of the day, such as eating, there was a realization of his presence. Taken together, the actions of that day on the road created a space in which the disciples could—in an instant—see the stranger for who he was and could recognize the once familiar "burning in their hearts."

It is our hope that the following chapters will shape similar contours for readers to recognize where and how we've unwittingly been co-opted by a consumer culture and what this is doing to teenagers, its effects on the coming-of-age process, and possible responses to counter it. We will start with a glance at the past, inviting the stranger on the road to serve as, if you will, a dialogue partner in critiquing consumer culture and putting present realities into context.

We believe we can and do find God in the midst of the ordinary world we live in, in spite of how commercial and mass-mediated it is. And although we can't share a meal with our readers, we *can* share a few stories of not only imaginative youth workers who are creating places for youth to emerge as adults with a sense of vocation and calling, but also teenagers' experiences in such places and how those have changed the scripts from which they live.

More Story Than Steps

This book is suggestive rather than prescriptive—more story than steps. No model is laid out on the following pages, and there is no fill-in-the-blank companion workbook to buy. Instead, our hope is that this slim volume will encourage readers to further pursue those themes that resonate with them and to a greater depth than is possible in this book.

What we aim to do is begin a conversation around three big ideas. Part One will examine the first two: (1) What consumer culture is doing to youth, and (2) What it means to grow up in a market-driven, consumer-saturated culture and how this experience needs to be reframed with an intentionally different ideology of youth.

Part Two examines the third big idea through the story of youth ministry as it has matured in practice and as a discipline within practical theology. Our aim here is to relate enough of the youth ministry story in order to begin asking how the rise of a culturally accepted version of adolescence—and the concurrent growth of a consumer-driven market economy—have impacted both the shape of youth ministry and the response of the church to adolescence. It offers a glimpse of the stories of teenagers, adults, and faith communities in the United States and Canada that have been impacted by an intentional vocational culture through the lens of Ministry Quest—a Lilly Foundation-funded project that has, to some degree, transformed churches, a seminary, and a denomination by "thinking vocationally with youth" focusing on call and vocational development. Functioning as a case study of sorts, Ministry Quest will inform the idea of how youth ministry and faith communities are situated to shape a significantly different ideology of youth—an alternative script for youth—and become places where a powerful antidote to consumer culture is lived out.

It is our hope that the chapters and themes of this book, when taken together, will suggest possibilities for practice in a "Youth Ministry 3.0" world.[9] What began during a conference as a conversation between the three authors soon evolved into a discussion at a Mexican restaurant about perspectives on culture, youth ministry, and books used in the development of youth workers. We talked about the work of sociologists James Côté and Anton Allahar and how it was shaping and informing our own thinking and practice of youth ministry. Côté and Allahar's original work, *Generation on Hold: Coming of Age in the Late Twentieth Century*, was a valuable introduction to the world of youth from an insightful and critical political-economic perspective. While we've used this text in our classrooms, we wondered why neither it nor its 2006 revision (*Critical Youth Studies*) had received wider use among those teaching about youth ministry in colleges, seminaries, and graduate schools.[10]

That discussion in the Mexican restaurant later turned into wider conversations, a sketchy outline for a new book, and an understanding that maybe there were some practical concerns not addressed in Côté and Allahar's text that may have kept it from the required reading lists of some youth ministry courses. Thus, this book is our attempt at blending the two—specifically ideas about the role that faith communities and youth ministries might play in the larger story of adolescence.

The work of Côté and Allahar has been a motivating force for us in the development and direction of this book, and we owe them a debt of gratitude, as well as a special thank-you to James Côté for his encouragement of this particular project when it was just an idea.

The stranger on the road took his companions back to the beginning to make meaning out of their present reality. We shall start there as well. If we are to understand teenagers' realities of "growing up cool" today, then we must begin at the beginning, if you will. And that's where we'll turn next with a look at the invention of adolescence.

TEENAGE:
A GENERATION
ON HOLD

1

GROWING UP THEN: THE CREATION OF ADOLESCENCE

We know that I have good posture, that I have broad shoulders, a high chest, hips and a derriere well rounded and prominent, and small feet. Within five minutes, I became a flat monster, emaciated, with sunken chest, and one shoulder higher than the other, which pushes everything else out of shape.

—Marie Bashkirtseff

The opaque glance and the pimples. The fancy new nakedness they're all dressed up in with no place to go. The eyes full of secrets they have a strong hunch everybody is on to. The shadowed brow. Being not quite a child and not quite a grown-up either is hard work, and they look it. Living in two worlds at once is no picnic.

—Frederick Buechner[1]

Marie Bashkirtseff was doing what many girls her age do—finding a source of comfort and the familiar by writing down her thoughts. Her early entries were not unlike any other teenage girl's thoughts regarding an uneasy relationship with her looks. One day she describes feeling "quite beautiful," and the next she believed she was "a figure not even Satan would recognize."[2] Other entries detail her dreams and desire for fame and celebrity. Confessions, frustrations, and dreams—which are not unlike the dreams, frustrations, and confessions of any teenager today—all found a home on the pages of Marie's diary. When Marie writes: "I dream of celebrity, of fame," we hear the shared preoccupations of the so-called "Facebook generation." Such ambitions were normally the playground of only the privileged, like Marie. But now they're embraced by every wannabe *American Idol* or reality show contestant, and they often find a home on YouTube—where the world watches an endless and diverse catalog of videos.[3]

So what makes the thoughts and diaries of seventeen-year-old Marie interesting? Well, they were written well over 100 years ago (back in 1875, actually). And some would say that's proof that teenagers have always been around, have always been a part of the social landscape, and have always been concerned with the same sorts of issues. This would be a common and widely held perspective.

But the word *teenager* wasn't in use then. Fast forward about 70 years to around 1944, and we'll see that the words *teenage* and *teenager* were part of the social landscape and used to describe the group of people between the ages of 14 and 18. And although the first usage of the terms was largely linked to marketing to that age group, the expressions stuck. "There's been a gradual, insidious change occurring in the very nature of adolescence over the past several generations," observe Joseph and Claudia Allen in their book *Escaping the Endless Adolescence*, "a change that has been stripping this period of meaningful work and of exposure to adult challenges and rewards, and undermining our teens' development in the process."[4]

We were entering the age of consumerism and the fast-paced expansion of pop culture. An age where work was replaced with consumption; where exposure to adult challenges and rewards was replaced with leisure, entertainment, and spending power. This was the time when teenagers were being noticed as a consumer market, not just as adolescents or (worse) delinquents. Consumerism would prove the counterbalance to rebellion and riot by redirecting the so-called disruptive energies of youth.[5] From this emerges another common view that people might have about adolescence and teenagers. After all, the thinking goes, the teenager rode in on the cresting waves of popular culture, specifically the emergence of rock 'n' roll, movies, and fashion.

Contradictory beliefs about teenagers and adolescence are common. Consider, for example, Thomas Hine's observation in *The Rise and Fall of the American Teenager* regarding just a few of the commonly held contradictions: Teenagers should be free to be themselves versus teenagers need many years of training and study, or teenagers know more about the future than adults do versus the belief that teenagers know nothing at all.[6]

Adolescence isn't some kind of blended version of child and adult, nor is it an expanded version of either stage. As it's now experienced, adolescence is an ongoing, socially constructed project that has a pretty clear beginning. However, its ending—the transition into adulthood— well, that's becoming more convoluted and confusing than it once was. Adolescence, as we know it, is a recent invention.

What You See Depends on Where You Stand

Social scientists who study adolescence don't speak in the classic terms of nature and nurture. The reality is that "adolescence begins in biology and ends in culture."[7]

From the standpoint of biology, it's clear (and stating the obvious) that biological maturation—puberty—is visibly universal and happens in every culture. Any general textbook on adolescence and most youth ministry books contain great detail on the physical characteristics and developmental theories of adolescence. So we won't repeat that here. However, the big trend to note relates to the age of onset of puberty, which has become younger in North America. This means that young people will reach sexual maturity earlier than they used to.

G. Stanley Hall, who first popularized the concept of adolescence back in 1904, saw biological maturation as the most significant thing going on in a young person's life.[8] And, as social historian Joseph Kett observed, from that moment on biology and the process of puberty became the basis for society to define, organize, and structure an entire age group.[9] Subsequently, a growing movement in psychological and psychiatric perspectives emerged that defined adolescence in terms of storm, stress, emotional distress, and problems emerging from the inner workings of the person. Hall's thinking on adolescence was embraced so fully and deeply that it influenced the growth and development of movements and cottage industries ranging from—

- the development of parenting manuals and the parenting resource industry, which was created to help parents manage their teenagers—particularly in the growing number of middle-class homes;

- movements to program the spare-time activities of young people in adult-sponsored youth organizations and clubs; and
- a critical need for more educators, as more and more youth were now entering the school systems, paired with the establishment of a growing vocational guidance movement to bridge the gap between the classroom and the workplace.[10]

The dilemma with a strictly biological (nature) perspective of adolescence is found in the simple fact that historical changes in Westernized society have gradually restructured the coming-of-age process in different ways. There simply is no "one way" that coming of age happens — despite the similarity in biological changes that take place throughout puberty.

In the past people in their teens were viewed as responsible and mature enough to strike out on their own and begin families. Paradoxically during that time in history, puberty occurred anywhere between two to four years later than it does now, yet our culture now attributes *less* maturity to the people of this same age range today.[11] Therefore, it would appear that something has changed to make adolescents more immature in spite of their accelerated biological development.[12]

Growing up, it seems, is also determined by culture. And on this ground stand sociologists whose perspectives are shaped by the lens of culture and the ideas of nurture. From this point of view, adolescence is more a product of social expectations linked with the teenagers' particular culture, and adolescence is seen as being a reality that is thrust upon those who are coming of age by forces outside of their control.

Despite this shared starting assumption, differences exist concerning which influences are most dominant in the structuring of the process. For some, adolescence is seen as a function of the social change brought about by industrialization. For others, it's the marginalization of youth that finds a home in subculture peer groups. And for still others, it's the regulation of social institutions and organizations (meaning the changes that occur, for example, in the family, educational institutions, and the workplace as mediated by mass media).

So does this mean that adolescence is only the result of social conditions? Any kind of reductionist thinking, or a reductionist point of view, wouldn't make sense. As Friedrich L. Schweitzer writes in *The Postmodern Life Cycle*, "But it makes sense to understand adolescence contextually by being aware of the social, historical, and institutional factors that define or even create the space in which the physiological and psychological processes can take place and in which they take on a certain shape."[13]

Wherever your point of view begins in regard to understanding adolescence, biology, culture, or points in between, the outcome is the same. Adolescence—as we know it now—is a recent invention and an experienced reality for those who are coming of age.[14]

Snapshots of Youth

From the time up to and throughout the eighteenth and nineteenth centuries, the gap between childhood and adulthood—what we call "adolescence"—didn't exist. Before industrialization changed the nature and location of the workplace, the home and family were the central elements of economic production. That meant that even five- and six-year-old children were expected to help with the household chores (for example, food preparation, caring for the animals, gardening, and so on).

Kids worked right alongside their extended family members, gradually taking on greater work responsibilities as they grew older. And outside opportunities such as attending grammar school and working in apprenticeships were chosen only if the family's circumstances allowed and if there were benefits to be gained by the whole family. Many children were sent to work for other families, sometimes relatives, where they'd do domestic or farm work or learn a craft.

Thomas Hine writes, "If a fourteen-year-old looked big enough and strong enough to do a man's work on a farm or in a factory or mine, most people viewed him as a man."[15] On the other hand, if a sixteen-year-old was slower to develop and couldn't do the work of a man, then he wasn't seen as being a man just yet. And similar commonsense logic prevailed for women. To be considered of marriageable age was a function of being ready for motherhood, which was determined by physical development, not age.

All of these factors caused the transition from childhood to adulthood to be relatively smooth. Young people were introduced to adult roles early on; they knew firsthand that their work experience or apprenticeship was relevant to their adult lives. They were already productive and contributing members of the household and society. And, for the most part, there wasn't a sense of alienation from the adult world.[16]

Adolescence as we know it today didn't exist, but all of that was about to change.

The concept of youth would change as industrialization initiated major migration from rural areas to cities. Economic changes ushered in a different kind of society—one based on a growing consumerism and mass production. In the ever-expanding cities, urbanization would alter the traditional structures of work, neighborhood, and family.

If you were to open a photo album containing pictures from the last 100 years, what might you see? One thing is sure: you'd see clear indications of how much things have changed.

A PRE-1930s PHOTO

There might be eight to ten people in this late 1920s photo—a mix of men, women, and children. But they obviously represent three generations of the same family. The picture might show them taking a break from working out in the field. They share a simple meal before everyone returns to doing the work of the farm. The image is one of simplicity; they don't appear wealthy, but they have what they need. You sense they enjoy what they're doing as well as each other's company.

The background of this moment in time is the fading of an agricultural way of life and the growth of an industrialized society. Family life is connected with work. People work together toward a common good, often sharing the tasks related to farm life. And it all happens more or less in the same place, so there's no need for any long-distance travel to and from work. Three generations living and working together is a common way of life. This will be the last photo of its kind in the family album.

Factors that would set the stage for the creation of adolescence were already at work. Joseph Kett writes in *Rites of Passage*, "Between 1890 and 1920 a host of psychologists, urban reformers, educators, youth workers, and parent counselors gave shape to the concept of adolescence, leading to the massive reclassification of young people as adolescents."[18] Industrialization produced machines that made farming less labor-intensive, so large families were no longer required to get the work done. As families began moving to the cities, their members—including many children and youth—found work in factories.

Then reformers later drafted and enacted child-labor laws. And around this same time period, compulsory education laws were introduced for children between the ages of 6 and 18. With child-labor laws removing minors from the workforce, more schools were needed to accommodate the growing numbers of students.

But reform didn't stop there. The juvenile justice system was created in response to the belief that youth were not being helped if they were punished the same as adults. So separate legal proceedings were introduced, which were intended to allow corrective measures instead of punitive ones. As a result of these various reforms and with additional cultural dynamics at work, adolescence emerged and would in fact comprise longer and longer periods of time, making it more difficult for youth to become adults.

A 1950s PHOTO[17]

In the center of this photo is a basic, simple car that's more than just a car. It's a symbol of personal achievement, mobility, and an increasing degree of affluence. The car fit what was inferred to be the ideal family size of two adults and two or three children. It was also the perfect size for and made it affordable to take road trip vacations to the lake or mountains. And unless the extended family, namely the grandparents, had their own car, it would be difficult for them to come along. So the oldest generation is now absent from this picture.

The background of this moment in time is the improved living conditions of the industrialized West in the period following World War II. Generally speaking, the family unit was now limited to just two generations—parents and children—and the so-called "nuclear family" designation was on the rise. And for many people, the workplace changed. The days of the family farm and the home being the center of work were now gone for most people. Thanks to the mass migration to the cities, the suburban commute was born.

Growing up during this time period was a much different experience than what took place in the preceding one. In the previous photo, it was assumed that young people would grow up and mature naturally through their connection with adults in the casual everydayness of life and work. But in this photo there was a growing tendency or an ideology to assume that the process of growing up was about a succession of problems, usually associated with sex and the social life, that parents must solve before youth could fully mature.

The school experience represented in the previous photo was seasonal because of the work associated with the farm, and classes were comprised of a whole range of ages mixed up together in one-room schoolhouses. However, in this time period, school was becoming the primary, full-time institution of adolescence. Classes were age-graded, which meant children were increasingly being isolated in a world of their peers for much longer periods of time, while well-meaning adults kept youth from any real and substantial responsibilities.

Adolescence as we know it was emerging. As Friedrich L. Schweitzer writes in *The Postmodern Life Cycle*, "One of the most important factors responsible for the historically late emergence of adolescence as a distinct stage within the life cycle is the scarcity of educational institutions in earlier history and cultures. Only with the introduction of mandatory schooling beyond the age of ten was there a social and institutional basis for adolescence to become a general experience in today's sense, and this kind of schooling is largely a twentieth-century innovation."[19]

With the growing affluence of the 1950s, adults provided their teenage children with money and the time to enjoy it through leisure. The growing entertainment industry noticed this new and growing market, and a relationship of dependence grew into a symbiotic relationship between media and youth. As Quentin J. Schultze, et al. write in *Dancing in the Dark: Youth, Popular Culture, and the Electronic Media*, "The media need the youth market, as it is called, for their own economic survival. Youth, in turn, need the media for guidance and nurture in a society where other social institutions, such as the family and the school, do not shape the youth culture as powerfully as they once did."[20]

A 1980s PHOTO

The promises of affluence have come to life in this particular photo of suburban life. The simple 1950s car has been replaced with a vehicle that not only provides transportation, but also signals the sophistication of a personal style and achievement. This photo contains the well-manicured lawn of the backyard, which also makes a statement about the family's level of accomplishment.

The smaller family size in this photo shows the stress of contemporary life. Both parents work, and there is no sign of involvement by extended generations or other family members. Kids experience less casual contact with adults except through regulated experiences such as school, clubs, and sports. Yet these have all become places of competition and cause youth stress of a different sort.

In the background of this moment in time is the wholesale acceptance of adolescence as a life stage. The now-entrenched social construction of adolescence owes much to three factors that converged in the growth of and movement to the urban-industrial society: the use of technology to improve productivity, the affluence generated by this change, and the dramatic movement of people to the cities (urbanization). These three factors dramatically altered societal structures to such an extent that they have significantly shaped what we now know as "adolescence."

THE BIG PICTURE

Consider what's changed between these three simple pictures: the rise of the nuclear family system, the movement of adolescents from the workplace to the school, adolescents' longer period of dependence on their parents, delayed marriage, the growth of commercial enterprises geared toward adolescents, and the diversification of work away from home to the development of a huge range of occupations pushing adolescents into more schooling.

As Don Richter writes in *Agenda for Youth Ministry*, "Simply put, youth and youth culture were invented because we needed them. With the shift from manual labor to machines and the emergence of a professional class requiring prolonged education, a new stage of life was defined for teenagers. Instead of learning a trade, running the farm or working in a factory, teenagers were expected—no required—to go to school. Instead of getting married and having children, teenagers were encouraged to abstain from or practice 'safe' sex."[21]

In *Teenagers: An American History*, Grace Palladino adds that the emergence of the teenager was not only deeply connected to the institutional identification through the requirement of high school, but also the economic identification through the greater consumptive capacities that teenagers increasingly had in the decades leading into—and now well beyond—the eighties.[22] As sociologist Tony Campolo concluded in his book *Growing Up in America*, "They buy because our consumer-oriented society has convinced them that buying establishes the fact that they've come of age and know who they are."[23] Adolescence had arrived in full force.

Fancy New Nakedness

This survey is not by any stretch an exhaustive account of the creation of adolescence. But we are in a position to raise the question as to how young people might experience the situation we are now in, namely this thing called adolescence. Obviously, different people in different places experience it differently. But one thing is sure: youth living in industrialized societies share a common experience of being considered non-adult, as well as being excluded and marginalized from a fuller, more significant participation in adult society. It leaves one with the sense that Buechner's observation—about adolescents being all dressed up in a fancy new nakedness with no place to go—is rather truthful.

This fancy new nakedness can take on the form of confusing and conflicting ideas about what teenagers ought to do and who and what they ought to become. For example, the biblical concept of vocation has been replaced by psychological and cultural ideas related to "getting a job" and "making money." We have lost the sense that vocation has as much to do with who one is and who one is becoming as it does with what one chooses as a career, work, job, or occupation.[24] From childhood on, young people are taught to listen, watch, and consume, rather than speak, participate, and act. Therefore—and this is a large part of the argument in this book—teenagers are valued not for their potential to contribute, but for their ability to consume and, more broadly, for what they achieve.

Another sense of the fancy new nakedness can be found in the many different ways in which youth cope and navigate the requirements of life in a postmodern world.[25] Our brief survey pointed to earlier time periods that were characterized by relatively static and predetermined social roles and identities. Ronald Koteskey reminds us that at one time identity was shaped and informed by one's culture (rites of passage), community (living in and relating to the "village"), religion (belonging to a culture and community often meant that one received a religious identity as well), and family.[26]

For teenagers today, identity is no longer a given; it's been classified as a developmental achievement. Therefore, one task of adolescence has become choosing and constructing an identity. The problem is that identity is more fluid and elusive for adolescents today, and it's further complicated by a consumer culture that's more than prepared to offer ready-made alternatives. Finding one's way through these vast images and values is complicated even more by the relative absence of adults and the lack of critical skills needed to navigate that journey.

Where We Now Stand

The few photos described in this chapter draw attention to moments in the creation of adolescence. Think of it as a short, general survey of the history of adolescence over the last hundred years that reveals the shifts that have altered the coming-of-age landscape. The shifting landscape has subjected teenagers to forces outside their control and increasingly to life in the margins. There is a theme that emerges from those forces—the abstractions of youth—which reveals several key dynamics in the shifting landscape of adolescence. What has changed from "growing up then" to now? The "abstractions of youth" reveal the following:

1. Youth were separated from *significant social roles* in communities. Youth roles are now limited to education, consumption, and peer relationships.
2. Youth were separated from *networks of care* in communities, including, to varying degrees, families and local authorities. Youth are now largely connected to and by peer relationships with little adult involvement.
3. Youth were separated from *attention to the common good*. Youth today are seduced by a mass-mediated culture to focus on stuff, celebrity, and the posh lifestyle.
4. Youth were separated from *faith communities*. Youth today are segregated *even within* faith communities into separate worship services and even specially designed buildings just for them.
5. Youth were separated from *expectations to fully attend to the call of God upon their lives* and from the sense of having any agency or power for shaping a better world or a belief on their part that God may actually call them to something greater than themselves. For many youth today there is no expectation or challenge to explore their abilities, let alone use them to shape a better world or a belief to which God calls them. The need for security and the desire for consumption drive their lifestyle and vocational choices.[27]

The story of the creation of adolescence reveals a fragmentation and alienation of the coming-of-age process in advanced industrialized societies like ours, and it needs to be understood within the context of a corporately driven consumer culture. We'll turn there now in order to understand "the making of the teenage market."

Discussion and Study Questions

1. In *Soul Searching* (Oxford University Press 2005), Christian Smith and Melinda Denton observe that (1) adults are preoccupied with problems, and (2) society creates a growing structural divide between youth and adults, both of which distract adults from the job of raising teenagers. We additionally suggest in this book that (3) our media-driven consumer culture (where purchasing power reigns supreme) contributes to a growing divide between youth and adults. How would you describe the impact of these three realities on how teenagers grow up? How would society describe what it means to grow up?

2. In regard to the "photo album" described in this chapter, if you were to add one more photo taken in 2010, what would it depict? Think about the youth you know, the community you're familiar with, and what you know about the shape and contours of North American culture. Describe the photo and unpack the details — what would we see?

3. Over the last 100 years, North American adolescents have been experiencing longer and longer periods of being "youth." Plus, a media-driven, consumer culture encourages an optional maturity in which adults are less likely to take on adult roles in relationships with teenagers (while trying to hang on to their own adolescence for as long as they can). In the end most youth simply are not part of the adult world and have little meaningful contact or relationships with adults. In the face of teenagers being so formally and informally segregated, what do you believe the long-term impact is for them?

4. When youth leaders (whether volunteers or those who study youth and youth ministry or any other practitioners) get together, the

conversation often turns to the promise and challenges of ministry with youth. What do you suppose the challenges are? What
must be done relationally and in ministry with—and on behalf of—
today's youth?

Try this . . .

Compare and contrast the portrayal of youth/teenagers in two movies
produced at least twenty years apart. What issues are revealed and how
are they treated in the films (e.g., personal identity, friendship, family
and/or intergroup relationships, appearance and body-image issues, sexual identity, cultural dissonance, etc.)? How do these portrayals resonate
with or differ from your own experience and how would they resonate
with or differ from youth growing up today?

2

GROWING UP NOW: THE MAKING OF A TEENAGE MARKET

Most people do not possess the historical perspective and knowledge to see how present-day society has been shaped and formed by self-interested groups of people acting over long periods of time, in this case decades and even centuries.

—James Côté and Anton Allahar[1]

Profit is useful if it serves as a means toward an end. Once profit becomes the exclusive goal, if it is produced by improper means and without the common good as its ultimate end, it risks destroying wealth and creating poverty.

—Pope Benedict XVI[2]

The coming-of-age process has undergone major change. One of the causes is the fact that teenagers have learned to consume rather than produce, which, ironically, is the polar opposite of what the transition to adulthood has been about for all of human history. Non-Western cultures and earlier generations of North Americans needed youth labor as a matter of course and contribution to family and community life. Today, however, youth are largely thought of as being "supplementary" to the functioning of society, and their consumption isn't given a second thought.

How did we get to this point? Here's the big idea: youth (and adult) consumption is linked to how our twenty-first century society is uniquely structured, and this structuring both pressures us and empowers us to act in ways no other civilization has ever acted.

Many youth are experiencing trouble through this contemporary structuring of today's society, and all youth face unprecedented pressure because of it. What's needed is a perspective that involves an understanding of how capitalism works, and more importantly an understanding of what its impact may be on youth—because we believe adults and faith communities hold great potential to alleviate many of the problems associated with coming of age today in this new marketed and consumer-mediated culture.

How Structuring "Coming of Age" Affects Youth Who Experience It

As you may recall from the last chapter, at the turn of the twentieth century, G. Stanley Hall and his first-of-its-kind analysis of the coming-of-age journey of North American youth provided the momentum for what was to come. Addressing the turmoil he witnessed among the young people of his time, Hall suggested that youth experience age-based, biologically induced stress (*Sturm and Drang*) that coincides with peak intellectual, physical, and social maturation and resulted in a period of inevitable savagery and unavoidable chaos in all adolescents' transition to adulthood.[3]

Hall's course of action was two-tiered: (1) Professional adult supervision, since youth were obviously chaotic and out of control; and (2) in contrast to the first tier, adult disengagement, since the situation was inevitable and the adolescents' difficulties would eventually pass. Perceptive youth workers have noticed that the momentum of Hall's analysis has produced exactly this type of intergenerational social arrangement that largely persists in North America today.

The arrangement Hall hinted toward was a cadre of professionals (social workers, educators, police officers, counselors, and so on) examining young people and prescribing "scientific" solutions to the problem of youth while nonprofessional, everyday adults (parents, grandparents, uncles, aunts, mentors, community members, church folk, and so on) pulled back and even withdrew their presence and waited for the tumultuous youth phase to pass. The chaos Hall witnessed and attributed (in many ways falsely) to biological causes was and continues to be exacerbated by social arrangements. The roots of this type of approach grew so deep that even today adults will distance themselves from the younger generation.[4]

About a quarter-century later, in 1928, much of what Hall suggested about inevitable youth angst came into serious disrepute through the work of anthropologist Margaret Mead. In her *Coming of Age in Samoa* study of a non-Western culture, Mead observed children and adults mixing freely and casually.[5] Grown-up tasks were foisted on youth as soon as they were able to handle them, and youth rose to the challenge. They felt a sense of belonging accompanied by self-esteem as mastery was achieved. Further, Samoan culture had an ethos of societal care, rather than a survival-of-the-fittest mentality. It seems that in this environment of adult nurture and support, where teen labor was valued and needed, young people thrived, and the transition to adulthood occurred as a natural, inevitable, and relatively stress-free process.

Mead's findings suggest an important sociological truth that we shouldn't forget about coming of age: Adolescent storm and stress is *not* inevitable. Rather, when it pervades the youth of a society, it's linked to how that society structures the coming-of-age process and who speaks the loudest and most forcefully about growing up. Over the twentieth century, the conception of adolescence has continued to shift as some social institutions retreated and lost their voices, while others emerged with louder voices and striking messages.

Five Social Institutions That Shape Children and Youth

A macro investigation of all societies identifies five essential social institutions that perform unique tasks and—through their interactions with and instruction of the young—provide key structuring norms that guide the eventual transition into adulthood. Over time the amount of influence each institution exerts can shift, resulting in certain beliefs emerging (and others receding) about what is important during the coming-of-age years. This then leads to the society accepting "common sense" truth about what it means to be a teenager and how growing up ought (or ought not) to happen. While the five institutions, generally speaking, have stayed fixed over time, both the content and the volume of each institution's message, relative to the other four institutions, have changed immensely. And their influence on how youth experience the teenage years has changed as well.

A look into most introductory sociology texts will highlight these five key social institutions that function in societies and serve essential tasks that intersect with the lives of the young.[6] (These institutions and their corresponding functions are described here in a general manner and aren't meant to be taken strictly or as exact across times and cultures. Since our purpose is to provide no more than a general overview of these social institutions, we are painting with a very broad brush.)

1. Extended Family—includes an intergenerational, extended network of people that follows bloodline and, at times, includes other children or adults of choice. The family's functions are providing a location for sexual activity and procreation, the nurture and primary socialization of children, and the care and reverence of the elderly. Key familial youth norms include dictates regarding whom to marry, how to manage sexual tension, how to participate meaningfully in the other institutional spheres, and how to treat family members—usually including a special reverence for both the very young and the elderly.

2. Religion or Faith Community—connects societal members to an overriding moral referent that gives meaning and value to everyday existence. It also provides a motivating sense of purpose while addressing the ultimate questions of existence. Further, faith communities act as "sacred canopies" that shield adherents from the trials and tribulations of a difficult world.[7] Key religious youth norms focus on how to connect with the transcendent and, as a result, how adolescents might live to maximize their everyday existence—and any afterlife.

3. Government—assists the society in preserving harmony within its borders and protects the society from outside threats. Government also provides a way of choosing and legitimizing leaders, as well as a method of creating laws and enforcing them for the purpose of regulating both group and individual life. Key governmental norms for the young focus on political participation, military service, and orderly personal conduct within the society.

4. Education—functions to train new members (both natural-born citizens and those who immigrate) about the mores, beliefs, and customs of the community. In more complex societies, this sector also prepares members for advanced types of work and, in partnership with the government, teaches citizenship building. Key schooling youth norms focus on educational participation for the sake of skill development and growth in civic responsibility.

5. Market Economy (including profit-driven popular culture)—involves an orderly production, distribution, and consumption of goods and services. Economic activity includes everything from extracting raw resources to processing finished products to the merchandizing of specialized goods and services. In advanced capitalist societies, these services have become branded, profit-driven, corporate-controlled, and pop culture-designed to confer identity for the young—a topic we will return to throughout the remainder of this book. Economic youth norms focus on participation in the production, distribution, and consumption process.

Table 1 provides a visual of the relative influence of these five key institutions over the last two centuries in North America, including the shifts over time and an estimation of future influence if the trajectories continue.[8] More specifically, it's estimating the degree of influence that each institution has on teenagers.

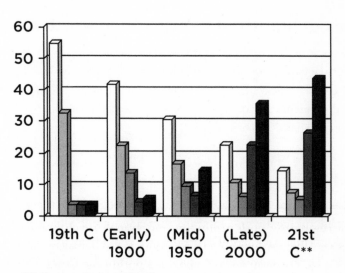

☐ Extended Family

▨ Faith Community

▨ Government

▮ Educational Sector

▮ Market Economy (including pop culture)

From the graph you'll notice patterns over time, as well as levels of relative sway at fixed intervals. For example, the role of government shifts in the lives of youth around 1900, when the state is a key player in legislating children out of the factories and mandating compulsory schooling. This fundamentally changed the youth experience as age-segregated classrooms became the norm, and it began the ongoing process of "institutionalization" of all children and youth.

And notice the big trend: the general decline in the influence of both family and religion, and the almost parallel growth of the market, media, and education influences over the last half-century. The market has moved from being almost a non-player to the ever-present force we see today. Since the way a society structures the coming-of-age process for adolescents is directly linked to how these youth experience growing up, this massive shift in institutional influence becomes important for youth advocates to understand. So let's look at the story of how advanced capitalism has come about.

Phases of Industrial Capitalism in North America

Our story of declining faith and rising consumerism involves a shift in the nature of capitalism. In his insightful book *Consumed: How the Markets Corrupt Children, Infantilize Adults, and Swallow Citizens Whole*, Benjamin Barber documents a transition from what he calls "productive" to "consumer" capitalism.[9]

EARLY INDUSTRIAL "PRODUCTIVE" CAPITALISM (PRE-1945)

When the Puritans sailed to America, they brought with them the "Protestant ethic" of hard work, forward thinking, public altruism, and strategic risk taking. An energetic, productive capitalism, as Barber calls it, took root. The focus was on producing goods and services that met real needs. It was believed that work was a divine calling to be balanced with minimal doses of leisure and that production and consumption should be tailored to supply and demand.

Even though workers were routinely exploited, often working in horrendous conditions, capitalists found satisfaction in producing goods and services that addressed the welfare of real human beings. Despite inconsistencies, there was a synergy between assisting individuals, building

communities, and making money. Market opportunities were determined by real needs. Saving and self-denial were virtues. Meanwhile,
debt, although necessary for the entrepreneur, was abhorred among the
citizenry. One lived within his means.

Ironically this ethos of frugal living and entrepreneurial risk taking—when fused with twentieth-century technological and scientific
advances—caused production to outpace consumption over time. Factories sprung up *en masse* in the early 1900s. This allowed the mass marketing of uniform new products. Further, scientific inventions brought a
host of options never before available. As Naomi Klein explains it in *No
Logo*, "Faced with a range of recently invented products—the radio, pho-
nograph, car, light bulb and so on—advertisers had [a pressing task] . . .
to change the way people lived their lives. Ads had to inform consumers
about the existence of some new invention, then convince them that their
lives would be better if they used, for example, cars instead of wagons,
telephones instead of mail and electric lights instead of oil lamps. . . .
these products were themselves news."[10]

Throughout this early capitalist period, new products continued to
emerge and some marketing took place. But the focus largely remained
on creating the good society. Even early corporations saw this as their
role. Corporations, modeling earlier European examples, were originally government charters that received legal powers (separate from the
individuals involved in it) to do some public good. For example, they'd
construct and operate a set of roads, extract and refine a desired raw
material such as timber, police and protect an outlying jurisdiction, or
produce and deliver electricity for a city.[11] This made perfect sense in a
rapidly expanding continent full of pioneers. Many corporations would
become hugely successful and prosperous and capable of monopolizing
the entire domain they engaged in—be that railroads, or steel, or the
postal service.

This new capitalist formula of "growing production + advertising =
growing adult consumption" roared during the 1920s. Then economic
activity stalled throughout the 1930s Depression era of credit crunch
and massive unemployment. The burden on consumers was, in part,
lifted with the New Deal and a brand-new level of government involvement in the economy. And then production quickly turned to the big war
effort of the 1940s.

MIDDLE INDUSTRIAL "INDIVIDUALIST" CAPITALISM (1945–1980)

In response to the massive postwar rebuilding effort, the economy sprang into high gear. Rising affluence during this time period provided a perfect nurturing environment for the seeds of individualism and materialism, which soon produced a consumer revolution. Growing wealth in the 1950s afforded people the opportunity to think and behave in new ways. The young adults of the time, scarred by the deep suffering of scarcity and war, resolved to build a society where future generations (especially their own children) wouldn't have to experience what they had.

With a growing standard of living and growing families, this became the era of the nuclear family. An expanding middle class had small but unprecedented levels of disposable cash, which created an opportunity for them to stylize their personal space and children in ways never dreamed of before. Previous luxuries—from telephones to refrigerators to television sets to children's bicycles—now became standard. And advertisers continued to introduce new products while encouraging more of the old. Consumerism was born. And an old, inconspicuous player—the corporation—gained prominence in society.

Corporations were positioned to grow exponentially, given the reconstruction demands and growing consumerism ethos of the postwar period. This new strength would unleash a darker side of corporations that had been inherent in their earlier legal language, which included providing a profit to their shareholders. A shift was underway within the ethos of corporations moving away from the idea of the common good and moving toward maximizing profits for shareholders. This meant that it made sense for corporations to continually find new markets to which products and services could be pitched. And in the late '40s, corporations discovered the youth "demo" in a big way.

Enter an age of direct advertising for fashion, music, and lifestyle options to the young. A mutually advantageous relationship between three entities resulted in a bonanza. First, there was the emergence of the largest youth population in history. Second, capitalism—an economic system that benefits from consumption—was firmly in place. And third, corporations strengthened by postwar optimism looked to flex their marketing muscle in new directions. It's no wonder that the discovery of a hot new market would let the genie out of the bottle in the form of direct marketing to young people.

Boomer children entered their adolescent years in intimidating numbers throughout the 1960s and 1970s. Their sheer numbers were overwhelming. This period was known for its self-expression, organic relationships, and experimentation—but also for youthful protest. It seemed that any rigid institutional structures or any institutional pressure that smothered this newfound evocative individuality was fair game for protest.[12] And this unleashed an unparalleled level of self-focus and blossoming creativity—something that marketers in the era of television were well positioned to co-opt. This symbiotic consumptive relationship continued through the 1970s and 1980s, and the stage was set for the consumer capitalist ethos that would permeate our present reality.

ADVANCED INDUSTRIAL "CONSUMER" CAPITALISM (1980 THROUGH THE PRESENT)

During the Thatcher and Reagan years of the 1980s, supply-side economics took root around the developed world. This philosophy stated that the government's role was to grease the capitalist wheels, and the benefits would flow throughout society. Less corporate taxation and regulation would increase economic activity and—via a "trickle-down" effect—the CEO, corporate elite, and even the worker would profit. This new approach unleashed a frenzy of deregulatory laws and free-trade agreements, thereby giving corporations new latitude to expand.

Throughout the 1980s and 1990s, a whirlwind of corporate and media mergers created an environment in which the same corporate conglomerate owned the product (such as cola), the means of communication (such as a television network, magazine, and newspaper chain), and the contract for the icon (sports star, musician, and so on) to endorse the product. Further, these conglomerates were now licensed to operate freely across national borders and essentially grow in size and strength. By the 1990s, the stage was set for the global advanced industrial capitalism of the twenty-first century that would create a hyper-consumerist ethos.

Free-trade agreements, corporate mergers, and global markets went hand in hand throughout the 1980s and 1990s with a key profit-producing strategy. Corporations could now lower labor costs by finding the cheapest locations to set up their factories. Profits could go up while employment would go down. North American manufacturing jobs could now be outsourced, and the middle class began to shrink. The young would now have greater difficulty finding good-paying employment than previous generations. This is a key reason for the prolonged nature of twenty-first-century adolescence[13] and what sociologists now call the emerging adulthood phase in the life cycle.[14]

In addition technological advances, such as the computer chip, were changing the workplace and positioning companies to lay off workers to increase their bottom lines.[15] Some corporations discovered that the profit bonanza of the future was even linked to getting out of production altogether. Branding would become the next big thing.

Branding involved creating and selling images and needs rather than products. A strategy of putting all of your research and development into the creation of an image, a lifestyle, a desired ethos that consumers would link with certain products associated with the brand.[16] The goal became manufacturing needs through highly refined advertising strategies that focused on consumer desire, the pursuit of cool, and consumption.

With an emerging branding culture, it was just a short step to the mass consumerism phase that Benjamin Barber suggests defines our culture with the following strategies:

PITCHING PRODUCTS AT CHILDREN—

In a world of too much stuff and too few buyers, children are a great solution. Thus, corporations focused their research on better understanding children, with one ultimate goal in mind: turning them into shoppers. If you get kids to buy early, they'll most likely develop a brand loyalty that will keep them coming back for more when they're adults.

HOMOGENOUS STRATEGY—

In an Internet-driven, shrinking world, the strategy is to sell the same products to youth no matter where they live. The rationale goes like this: Kids generally do the same things—play, snack, go to school, and (increasingly) learn English. Since they're doing the same things, wouldn't the most profitable marketing strategy be to pitch them all the same stuff?

FOCUS ON CREATING A "CONSUMPTIVE ETHOS" FOR THE ELDERLY—

By encouraging adults to remain "youthful," there is a greater tendency that they'll buy toys well into their senior years. This strategy involves undermining the voices that critique a consumer culture while reshaping educational, religious, and civic institutions in support of a consumptive ethos.

TORRENT OF IMAGES AND SOUNDS PERMEATING EVERYTHING—

How do you pitch products to preschool kids? How do you sell globally to international youth? How do you maintain adults as lifelong consumers? In a word: media. It gets the word out everywhere and in every way and by any means possible—from corporate programs in schools to political messaging in video games; from Internet commercials to product placement in movies; from youth-research websites to giant billboards in town squares; from logos on public transportation to the renaming of community complexes. Media is unlimited—an unending stream of manufactured images and sounds.[17]

Yet in spite of these strategies, and perhaps because of them, there is now a growing segment of both the adolescent and adult populations that is finding consumerist tendencies to be unsatisfying and is questioning the ethics and sustainability of the present ethos. In sociological terms, the corporate "manufacture of their consent" is leading to a corresponding "manufacture of dissent." Or to state it in theological terms, God is at work. The unintended consequence of the marketed narcissism is a deep desire for a more fulfilling lifestyle, as is evident in the recent increase in youth awareness and involvement in environmental causes, social justice movements, local acts of compassion, thirty-hour famines, and anti-consumerism campaigns, to name a few.

What Is Advanced Capitalism's Impact on Youth?

Advanced capitalism is decreasing workplace opportunities linked to sweeping economic changes associated with globalization. Instead of a range of good jobs with good benefits, there now are fewer employment opportunities. This paves the way for many young adults to delay their entry into adult roles—such as getting married, starting a career, owning a home, and having children. A clear trend throughout the 1980s, 1990s, and 2000s indicates a lengthening of the amount of time between the dependency of childhood and the independence of adulthood. The full age group transition now goes from age ten through the mid–thirties for many people—and it comes with all sorts of anxiety along the way.

This prolonged transition leads to youth marginalization. Be it political, educational, social, or economic—youth actually are on the fringes of those four spheres in the twenty-first century, and this amounts to a "generation on hold." Further, many youth and young adults experience false consciousness. They're simply unaware that current conditions were socially produced, and that these conditions—fueled by a consumer culture—now represent a "new normal."

In the next chapter, we'll look more closely at the new normal using what C. Wright Mills called "sociological imagination." We'll introduce a way of observing and making sense of how consumer structures contribute to teen marginalization and frustration with growing up branded.

Discussion and Study Questions

1. Have you seen the adults in your context defer to professionals when it comes to understanding and meeting the needs of youth? Discuss how G. Stanley Hall's 100-year-old idea (that non-professional adults don't have what it takes to meet the needs of youth) might be partly to blame? How can we reactivate the role of adults (i.e., parents, grandparents, adult mentors, volunteer youth workers, etc.) in the lives of our youth?

2. Do the findings of Margaret Mead (that some cultures have non-stressful transitions to adulthood that are associated with the need for teen labor, stable adult identities, and an ethos of societal care) surprise you? How might her findings provide insight for youth work, ministry, and faith communities? What lessons might adults take from Mead's insights to reduce the stress placed upon teens in their spheres?

3. Look at the table on page 37. In what ways have you observed parents and religious leaders struggling to gain audience with youth compared to educators and the marketplace? Discuss practical ways families and faith communities can proactively—without being simplistic or reactionary—turn up the volume of their messages.

4. Benjamin Barber suggests that advanced capitalism involves four strategies impacting the teenagers you work with. Reflect on how your youth:

   • were turned into shoppers as children.
   • are pitched global products that bypassed their cultural uniqueness.

- have grown up with a modeled consumerism.
- experience a constant surge of images and sounds designed to pitch products.

Try this . . .

Walk inside a shopping mall and observe the diverse means by which adolescents' attention is targeted by advertisers, media, magazines, retailers, and others. What do they (i.e., those in the business of persuading adolescents to change their habits or priorities in some way) know about teenagers and their development that we may not be paying attention to? How do they apply that knowledge to bring about those changes? How would you counter it?

3

GROWING UP BRANDED: WHAT ADVANCED CAPITALISM IS DOING TO YOUTH

The low status of young people means that an entry level into adulthood is inaccessible to them. They are not permitted to enter the community as adults. If you don't give them an opportunity to be meaningful participants in the construction of objects or community or houses or books or ideas or anything like that, well, then you're only left to be a consumer. And if you're only left to be a consumer, then you've got to consume.

—*All the Right Stuff*, a documentary by the National Film Board of Canada[1]

For those of us who live deeply immersed in the branding economy, we make an identity for ourselves, and an identity is made for us, by our relationship to consumer goods . . . Never before have young generations had to contend with such an intensive culture of corporations who want to sponsor this identity work for us.

—Tom Beaudoin[2]

Three Stories

STORY 1

Something new was happening in gym class. A student, whose father is a superintendent of schools, shared the following incident that happened in one of the elementary schools under her father's jurisdiction. As some fourth-grade girls were changing into sweats before P.E., those girls who were not wearing thongs were being teased. Being teased in fourth grade is nothing new. But what *is* new is being teased for not wearing what used to be considered adult underwear.

Think for a minute about any fourth-grade girls you might know. What comes to mind? Maybe you see promising soccer players, ballet dancers, or piano players. Maybe you envision kids who are quick at science or inquisitive about math and social studies. Maybe you see artists or emerging actresses. Or maybe you see kids who are loved by their parents, family, and friends—or kids living in more difficult circumstances.

Whatever you see, we can probably agree on this: no young girl should be told by anyone—anywhere—that the size or style of her underwear is what matters. How can we make sense of and then wisely respond to this age compression that is affecting an entire generation?

STORY 2

"Monday morning at 9 a.m. sharp—not a minute later. Be there *exactly* as the store opens." This very detailed instruction set into motion our second story. I was told to go to a certain store that my teenage son frequents and take along a copy of an exclusive invitation and a $200 deposit. He also informed me that had it not been a school day, he would have done the transaction himself. Then over the next several days, he persistently quizzed me to make sure I did not forget a single detail.

So what was the important event? My son had been monitoring the EB Games website, and 9 a.m. Monday morning was the first possible moment one could pre-order a much-anticipated Nintendo Wii gaming console. When the day finally arrived, I went to the store and plunked down ten crisp $20 bills.

Then I noticed that one of my son's rather ecstatic tenth-grade friends was also in the store. Talking to him I discovered that his father had dropped him and a friend off the night before. They'd slept outside the store (in the snow), guaranteeing him the status of being the first person in his high school to receive PlayStation 3—a $700 alternative gaming package pre-released the same day as Wii.

Eleven hours spent outside on a cold night, a significant financial investment, a day of school skipped, and subsequent weeks of time spent learning to master the console and new games. Again, we ask the question—why?

STORY 3

"This is probably unlike any email you have ever received . . . I am all alone" is how her email began. A student, she was every bit the motivated, disciplined, and energetic young woman. She then went on to share a story about her growing anxiety as both she and her recently graduated fiancé (both with undergraduate degrees) were in the middle of a massive crisis of confidence concerning their futures.

Unable to find work in his area of study, the fiancé had moved into the basement of his mother's home located in a large urban center. And then he'd slipped into a quiet depression and was actually scrounging the neighborhood for bottles to cash in.

And the former student was growing increasingly anxious about how she'd be able to turn a degree into gainful employment and how all her goals of marriage, family, home, and meaningful work could be realized. There was a disconnect between her and the adult world, which meant she was totally unaware of the many emotional, spiritual, educational, medical, and workplace resources that were available to help ease the transition into adulthood.

The tween who's teased for not wearing the "right underwear"; the teen who spends a school night camped out in the snow in order to beat his peers to the next piece of cool; and the isolated young woman who looks like she has it all together on the outside but is very confused on the inside—how do we make sense of these stories? Disciplines such as developmental psychology, education, history, and theology have provided compelling insights on human behavior and development that have informed and shaped the discipline and practice of youth ministry. This book will now introduce another helpful discipline. To help us make sense of these stories—and the stories from our own interactions with teenagers—we turn to the field of sociology and the shaping of a sociological imagination.

Using One's Sociological Imagination: Linking Youth Stories to Society's Stories

For most adults who care about youth, it's second nature for us to jump in to help specific individuals like those mentioned in the stories above. As an educator it would be instinctive to admonish the perpetrators while consoling those who were teased in the fourth-grade girls' gym class. As a parent of teenagers or as a youth worker, it would seem to be common sense to steer the teen you encountered in a gaming store to head back to school or, at the very least, inquire about it. As a professor who receives a distressing email from a student, you'd naturally set up a meeting to listen to her story and brainstorm possible resources and directions. However, tween bullying, teen truancy, and young adult quarter-life crises will continue unless both adults and teens understand—and in some ways reshape—the social environments in which these issues take place.[3]

We must learn to see the range of possible troubles that youth may face—but with a new imagination. Our gaze needs to encompass not only the school and family setting, but also something more fundamental—the way in which our advanced capitalist society creates an environment where *being sexy*, *being cool*, and *being credentialed* have become the drivers and the engine of a marketed youth culture that's at once powerfully attractive and potentially destructive to youth.

C. Wright Mills calls this way of seeing "sociological imagination."[4] We can learn to fully understand the personal lives of individuals by *also* making sense of the large-scale structuring of their societies and then discerning the extent of the stress-producing influence that these structures exert. To put it another way, the private anxieties of fourth-grade girls, tenth-grade boys, and college seniors are closely linked to how an advanced industrial consumer society structures opportunities and provides roles that create value for its youthful citizens.

Youth-Hood: A Generation on Hold

To develop our sociological imagination, we lean on James Côté and Anton Allahar's political economy perspective.[5] Once we see where youth are situated, we can begin to understand why they react the way they do and, more importantly, who is influencing their reactions. According to Côté and Allahar, young people in societies such as ours are *a generation on hold*. You may have heard that age thirty has become the new twenty.

Key markers of traditional adulthood—such as first marriage, first child, first home, and meaningful employment—are being delayed in countries all across the Western world.[6] Furthermore, the adolescent years aren't giving emerging young adults the skills, opportunities, and mentoring they need to advance into fulfilling adulthood.

Sociologists have a term for this phenomenon: "Youth-hood." It's generally framed by two postures—the very playful, "I have no responsibilities" take on life; and the more dutiful, "it's all up to me" approach. Yet both are ultimately inadequate because youth aren't receiving the skills they'll need to become responsible, fully mature adults.

From the beginning of civilization, our understanding of youth was one of transition—that time and space in which we moved from child-*hood* to adult*hood*. Now, however, adolescence has become a chosen destination (for some teens, anyway). In our culture it's entirely possible to become Peter Pan-like and never grow up. National social trends data indicates as much, reporting that most eighteen- to thirty-four-year-olds have passed through fewer adult transitions than people their age thirty years ago.

In our late modern, commercially mediated world, adulthood is feeling the squeeze. What was once a destination marked by signposts such as leaving home, graduating from school, holding a full-time job, or being in some kind of committed relationship is now fodder for the quarter-life crisis and film script ideas about twentysomethings. If what it means to be an adult is fuzzy and the transition is hazy, then leaning into and preparing for adulthood becomes an endeavor that is up for grabs. In such a world, apathy is seen as cool, having "things" sets you apart, and the right credentials will get you that "oh-so-perfect job."

But when you turn down the noise and step back from the fray, an unsettling reality hits. They have more stuff, but they're less sure of themselves. From a political economy perspective, young people are a class without power. They're disenfranchised economically, educationally, politically, and socially.

ECONOMICALLY: CONSUMING AND DEPENDENT

Economically, many youth feel they don't have the necessary skills, nor do they know the required steps to move from their position of dependence to one of meaningful work as productive and contributing members of their communities. Yes, many are working. But their jobs are largely service industry, part-time, dead-end, minimum wage, and with no benefits and little chance of long-term advancement. "McJobs," they're often called.

So in young adulthood, meaningful work is a source of frustration, but the seeds of this problem are planted much earlier. During the tween years, most youth receive a hefty allowance from their parents but with few saving and spending guidelines. As tweens move into the teen years, many will add part-time work to their weekly routines. For many youth, however, this work is often disconnected from any responsibility to produce a financial future or emerge as a productive adult. "I don't pay rent," says Brandon in the Canadian documentary *All the Right Stuff,* "My money is 100 percent disposable, so naturally I dispose of it."[7]

Most youth remain highly dependent on their parents for basic food, shelter, and clothing needs well into their young adult years. A key reason for this prolonged dependency is the expectation and need for higher education.

EDUCATIONALLY CREDENTIALED: FEW WINNERS AND LOTS OF LOSERS

Côté and Allahar suggest that what we have is a competitive, Texas Hold 'Em poker-style educational system in which everyone has to ante up, but there are more losers than winners.[8] Consider this claim: over the 13 years of K–12 formal schooling, each youth antes up almost half her waking hours for 190 days each year. Furthermore, as teens make this massive time investment into their futures, they are age segregated. And, ironically, very few adults in their communities will naturally interact with them during their quest to prepare for the adult world.

Yet, by the time these young people should be arriving at their senior prom, approximately 20 percent of them have fallen off the educational wagon and dropped out of school. By this time all youth, regardless of their prior academic success, are firmly entrenched in credentialism— the idea that good credentials secure a good future. And the pressure to pursue further education continues.

While approximately 80 percent of high school students expect to graduate from college,[9] many do not achieve this goal. (This is the case in both the United States and Canada.) As of 2003, 49 percent of Canadians ages 25 to 34, for example, were credentialed either by a college (21 percent) or a university (28 percent).[10] This means that slightly more than half of a nation's twenty-five- to thirty-four-year-old population is moving into young adulthood somewhat deprived of the credentials viewed as necessary for their success. This group is referred to in sociological circles as *the under-researched forgotten half*, and anecdotal evidence suggests there is a high rate of emotional distress among them.

However, for the one in two that does graduate, another hurdle needs to be faced. For the vast majority of careers, the number of credentials required has inflated. Take secondary-school teaching, for example. In 1955, you could receive a teaching certificate via a six-week summer school course. In 1969, it took a two-year teaching diploma. In 1984, a four-year bachelor's degree in education was necessary to get the same teaching position. And today, many universities have added a fifth year to the teaching degree. Despite this educational inflation, advocates argue that the university degree is still a good investment.

They have a point. The average lifetime earning power of someone with a university degree is $1 million higher than that of someone with only a high school diploma.[11] Advanced schooling pays off for many, but here's the paradox: according to Côté and Allahar's analysis, for every one job requiring a university degree, we are producing two university graduates. And many community college diplomas do not translate into full-time, high-paying work.

Have you ever wondered why so many post-secondary grads still work at Starbucks or your favorite independent java joint after graduation? Yes, there are many who hit the jackpot through their educational pursuits. But underemployment, anxiety, and frustration plague those who lose the credentialism game. A new reality is that before most young people turn 25, they have to deal with the disillusionment of their educational dreams.[12]

POLITICALLY: A DEGREE OF APATHY THAT TRANSLATES INTO DIMINISHED VOICE

Politically, youth aren't faring very well, either. The good news is that a growing number of social analysts point to a globally aware and socially active disposition among the young. The Obama presidential campaign certainly demonstrated that new technologies and a compelling message of hope and change can rally a younger generation to political action. However, the jury is still out on whether or not these factors have created a lasting shift. For one thing, adolescents are deprived of the right to vote until the age of 18. Hence, they show little interest in the formal political process as teenagers.

According to recent data, low numbers of American and Canadian teens claim to be interested in or active in politics. Even among the twentysomething crowd, almost one in two has little or no interest in politics. James Côté explains that we live in a society based on self-interest, and groups will form and lobby for their own interests in the political forum. No one speaks for young people in the political process, and young people are not advocating for themselves. Thousands of decisions are made each day that affect them (such as wages for certain jobs, the cost of education, priorities for public perks, etc.) and are made without their consideration. Further, without advocacy comes lack of voice, and no voice leads to exploitation. A case can be made that youth are one of the few remaining societal groups that we're allowed to exploit.[13]

SOCIALLY: PEER-ORIENTED AND A TRIBE APART

Socially, most youth are disenfranchised. First, the vast majority of youth don't have significant adult contact. The tacit assumption on the part of most adults is that in their drive toward autonomy and independence, teenagers just don't want a connection with adults. And this idea "that most teens don't want or need strong relationships with adults," according to Joseph Allen and Claudia Worrell Allen in their book *Escaping the Endless Adolescence*, "is perhaps the single most damaging belief we hold about adolescents today."[14] Youth are further segregated by age or grade in schools and while hanging out in social settings. Spending a massive amount of time with their peers develops a peer orientation, rather than an adult one, which continues to make interaction with the adult world awkward.[15]

In the words of Patricia Hersch, teens are a tribe apart—not because they left us, but because we left them. This generation is spending more time alone than any in other recent history.[16] Without adult contact it is little wonder that adolescence is prolonged and confusing for the younger generation. All the while, there are forces at work that make teen consumption a key priority. To understand this reality, we turn to the work of Noam Chomsky and a concept he developed called the "manufacture of consent."[17]

How Youth Consent to a Consumer Agenda

According to Chomsky, "the major decision-making power in our advanced capitalist society at a macro level about things like investment, production, distribution, and marketing are in the hands of a concentrated network of major corps, conglomerates, investment firms who own media and play an overwhelming role in terms of what happens in society."[18] These conglomerates own the means of production that create the stuff people buy. They own the communication line that creates an awareness of the products they have to offer. In addition, they also own the contracts of the celebrities hired to pitch those products to consumers. Through the synergy created by highly specialized production, sophisticated advertising, and strategic endorsement, this group is able to "manufacture the consent" of the rest of society so their corporate interests can be met. In this social environment, propaganda is an integral part of democracy, and corporately driven marketing practices—such as "cool hunting"—emerge in youth culture. In order to mask the disenfranchisement of youth (and to ensure that youth don't rise up against their exploitation), it is necessary for youth to experience a long indoctrination into accepting the existing power structures as normal, natural, and benign.

From a very young age, children learn to define themselves in capitalist terms as an individual, autonomous, rational, self-seeking, and cost-benefiting consumer.[19] And the states, schools, media, advertisers, families, and even religious institutions tend to reinforce this message. According to social analysts, youth become indoctrinated into a capitalist ideology, which goes something like this:[20]

1. Society is innately benign, while individuals are innately inadequate.
2. The economy functions in the interest of the average person.
3. The educational system is based on merit.
4. Youth get the jobs and future they want if they behave and work hard.
5. The best way for youth to earn favor and find fulfillment is to consume things.
6. Individuals, not the system, are responsible for any regrets they have in their lives.
7. If anything bad happens, don't worry—it can be fixed with more consumption.

This ideology is subtly found in advertising, curriculum, political rhetoric, some religious discourse, and the "common sense" cultural approaches to growing up. The message also makes its way into movies, magazines, and newspapers. As a result, our young people come to believe that they control their own destinies. However, few realize the degree to which their actions are shaped by corporate interests. According to research from a national youth survey, almost 90 percent of teens state that their own will power has a great deal of influence over them, but only 36 percent feel that people in power have this same degree of influence.[21]

Most youth honestly believe it's up to them to get where they want to go, it's their responsibility to make the most of it, and that with a good work ethic (something many of them haven't been taught) they can get there. While a sense of individual responsibility is refreshing, there is a downside. According to a political economy perspective, young people have been conditioned into a state of false consciousness. They don't recognize the influence because it is so pervasive.

Marketed Identities

Adolescents live in an environment in which much of their culture constitutes a consumer culture. Big business markets fashion, music, art, new technologies, and other consumer items. These goods all have in common an identity-conferring quality. In other words, you become "someone" or get into the "in" group by consuming or possessing a particular item. The disenfranchisement, marginalization, and disposable income of youth make them target markets for this identity manipulation. And while youth consume, corporate "cool hunters" look for the next great thing and market strategies focused on the bottom line.

Corporations can arbitrarily set trends, create new products, make aging ones obsolete, or keep changing what's "cool" year after year—and they do it all through the media they own.[22] Take gaming consoles as an example. Once, Nintendo 64 and the popular *Super Mario 64* game were hot, then along came PlayStation 2 complete with *ATV: Offroad Fury* and other cool games. This, however, was also only a temporary fix before the highly touted and much-marketed Xbox and its famed *Halo* and *Halo 2* hit the shelves. Twelve months later a new, more advanced Xbox 360 was added to the collection. And less than a year after that, the Nintendo DS handheld gaming console and the revolutionary Wii, complete with

Zelda and the Mario package, were in high demand. Then *Halo 3* arrived and so did . . . well, you get the idea. And along the way, identities are being shaped—in subtle ways, to be sure—by manufactured trends and "product tie-ins" marketing campaigns. This identity manipulation is done without conscience.

Let's reflect again on the stories from the beginning of this chapter. Utilizing our sociological imagination, let's unpack the macro realities connected to the personal troubles experienced by a tween being teased for not wearing a thong, or the teen choosing to camp out in front of a store to pick up the latest gaming console, or the anxiety of an isolated university graduate as she contemplates marriage and career.

According to Erik Erikson, identity formation is a key task during adolescence. In tribal and most non-Western societies, identity was conferred by involving a community of adults and some elaborate rites of passage, such as the bar mitzvah. However, in advanced industrial societies, identity formation is less structured. Just how one becomes "acceptable" is left unclear and murky at best. In this environment, youth are prone to manipulation by corporate enterprises eager to provide them with an identity for a price.

One such identity that was marketed to girls was the midriff: "You are your midriff. You are what you wear. Your identity is tied up in your appearance. Your body is your best asset; flaunt your sexuality even if you don't understand it."[23] So retailers sell fishnet stockings and padded bralettes to younger girls.

On the other hand, the identity being sold to boys is that of the "mook"—that loud, crude, testosterone-driven character found on MTV programs, frozen in permanent adolescence. As a result, boys engage in marketed sexual innuendo and *Jackass* humor throughout their school years—sometimes even well into their twenties.

In a marketed world, identity formation takes on the form of identity *manipulation* as a narrowly defined image of womanhood (midriff) and manhood (mook) are introduced to children and youth. Growing up inside this blizzard of messages from both retailers and the media can be confusing. It's as if a consumer virus has attached itself to the prolonged moratorium space that defines adolescence. And that virus has, in a sense, infected the growing-up or coming-of-age process to such a degree that the adult tasks that were so commonly learned during earlier generations now literally seize up. What's the antidote? That's the question we'll attempt to answer in the next chapter.

Discussion and Study Questions

1. C. Wright Mills' sociological imagination suggests that the private troubles of youth are linked to macro-social forces such as capitalist consumption. What are the biggest troubles of youth in your group? How are they linked to the pressure to be sexy, cool, or credentialed?

2. The youth "years" represent the transition from child*hood* through youth and into adult*hood*. How have you witnessed youth having trouble making this transition? Why are they finding it hard?

3. James Côté and Anton Allahar suggest that advanced capitalism marginalizes youth economically, educationally, politically, and socially. Think about the youth you know. In what ways are they consuming but not contributing; credentialed but disillusioned; politically apathetic and socially separated from adults? In what ways do these conditions make it difficult to find a meaningful transition into adulthood?

4. We began this chapter with this preliminary quotation: "If you don't give [youth] an opportunity to be meaningful participants in the construction of objects or community or houses or books or ideas or anything like that, well, then you're only left to be a consumer and if you're only left to be a consumer then you've got to consume." Are youth in your context—and youth that you have known—given meaningful opportunities to be productive? If so, how? And in what ways?

Try this . . .

Gather a group of three or four youth for a conversation and ask them if they notice how advertisers push their consumerism buttons and drive their consumerist lifestyles. Ask what, if anything, does this do to them and their peers—are youth desiring more? If so, what do they desire? Can they detect any sense of a consumer mindset in how church or their faith communities are structured—and if so, in what ways? What do they suppose this does to people and in regard to how faith is practiced? To what extent is the mook (boy stuck in adolescence, crude) and the mid-riff (adolescent girl becomes adult sex object) the norm in their schools? Ask how those identities might shape the manner in which adults relate to them as teens. Ask about why it seems girls are given a kind of adult status while boys seem reduced to a quirky adolescence. Finally ask for their advice regarding how you can best support and challenge them as they become adults in this kind of culture.

4

AN ANTIDOTE: A NEW IDEOLOGY OF YOUTH

A deep joy is like the compass which points out the proper direction for your life. One should follow this even when one is venturing on a difficult path.

**—Advice from a mentoring priest
to eighteen-year-old Mother Teresa[1]**

You are not what you do. You are not what you have. You are not what people say about you. You are the beloved sons and daughters of God.

—Henri Nouwen[2]

In *Practicing Discernment with Youth*, David White speaks convincingly about the tension that exists between the gospel and the cultural realities of adolescence.[3] At one point he uses the metaphor of trying to grow an oak tree inside an orange crate to illustrate the strain of being a normal teenager and how that precludes many of the ways of being faithful. For teenage life, as we all know, doesn't tend to move in the direction of simplicity, contemplation, silence, discernment, and so on. Either the tree will burst out of the crate and grow tall, or the tree will grow clearly distorted and dwarfed by what surrounds it. White suggests that much like the crate limits the growth of the oak tree, the constraints of adolescence distort such things as becoming an adult and the formation of faith. So the question is this: Are teenagers bursting out of those constraints? Or are they being distorted and dwarfed by what surrounds them?

White wonders what it would be like to have the responsibility of tending that growing oak tree in the crate and how very frustrating it would be. He then connects that frustration to the frustration of youth advocates who've been trying to disciple and cultivate a growing faith in youth within the confines of a socially constructed life stage called "adolescence." Oftentimes it seems that in spite of more and better resources or even more and greater hard work, things improve only in minor ways.

White's conclusion is relevant to our discussion as he observed that youth need youth workers "who dedicate whatever resources they already have to understanding and resisting the distortions of culture and living into the way of Jesus—and helping youth to do the same."[4]

Youth need youth workers who understand the distortions of a socially constructed version of adolescence—and offer an alternate version. Youth need youth workers who not only understand the distortions of a youth culture that is heavily mediated by a consumer-driven agenda whose target is teenagers, but also offer an alternate agenda. Youth need youth workers who understand the distortions of growing up in a youth culture that has disconnected them from relationships with adults (and the wisdom of adults), and in its place celebrates fame and celebrity. "If youth ministry is to break out of its cultural captivity," writes White, "we must frame our work in a different way."[5] That is the subject of this chapter—to examine what ministry to youth would look like if it were framed differently.

Before we do that, though, we need to unpack the experience of youth as it's mediated by a consumer-driven agenda supported by advanced capitalism's belief about what it means to be young. This belief, as we'll discover, describes teenagers as consuming, self-absorbed, peer-oriented, and rebellious—a pretty small and constraining crate to be sure. And this belief is expressed in the form of an ideology.

An ideology is a system of beliefs that claims to be true. These "truths" do not need empirical evidence to back them up—they're just accepted as "common sense." "Everyone knows . . ."—or so the thinking goes. But once the thinking is fixed in a community's mind, it tends to become a self-fulfilling prophecy born out in reality. And when it becomes fixed in reality, it reinforces in people's minds that the reality must be so. In our advanced capitalist consumer culture, this becomes our "common sense" way of thinking about adolescence. Another way to think about this ideology is akin to a virus—an advanced, capitalist virus.

Most of us are familiar with biological viruses like the ones that cause the common cold or the flu. They're not like bacteria or germs in that they aren't living things. They are protein-encased shell-like things that contain genetic material. The virus uses its shell to latch onto a healthy cell, and then it injects its own genetic material into the healthy cell. The virus code then mixes and competes for control with the healthy cell's genes. If it wins, it changes the way the cell functions.

The "shell" of the advanced capitalist virus could be any of those things that are used to capture our attention, from advertising to branding to a host of other attention-grabbing techniques. Once it's attached, the virus releases its ideological code, and this code permeates the way we think about certain things or, more specifically, "what" we think. In this case it affects what we think and believe about teenagers. The virus also informs the activities of young people all across North America and the attitudes of the adults who spend time with them. And because this "code" informs and shapes the lives of youth and the beliefs of adults, we tend to believe it just has to be so.[6]

As youth live their lives shaped by this ideological code, it reinforces the beliefs and the virus continues to work, multiply, and grow stronger. Over time and in subtle ways, teenagers stop knowing who they really are, and the basic functions connected with growing up—skill development, identity, intimacy, and contribution to others—are slowed and distorted. Life doesn't work as it was intended to, and youth find themselves living in a very small orange crate—held down by ideologies and feeling lifeless inside.

The "ideological code" that youth receive in our consumer-mediated culture is four-pronged:

Prong One: Youth as Consumers

Youth are viewed by our advanced capitalist system as buyers of goods and services. Not only that, but they're also aggressively targeted as both a present and future market. Their value stems from the understanding that they have large, disposable incomes that they're more than willing to part with for things that are cool, look good, sound good, or taste good—all generating profit for the makers of these products and images. This understanding masks the reality that youth are also connected to the gears of the system. After all, they're the ones who provide the indispensable labor force to run the fast-food chains and big box stores (and possibly even work in the sweat shops in developing countries). The current ideology of youth tends not to focus on this fact, however. Rather, it continually keeps the eyes and minds of teenagers focused on consumption.

Prong Two: Youth as Self-Absorbed

If youth are to be a target market, it makes sense that they should be focused on their own dreams, needs, and desires while ignoring the aspirations of others. A self-oriented, individual focus within an atmosphere that's geared toward the survival of the fittest tends to encourage personal consumption. What the advertisers won't address is the role they play in manufacturing the dreams and desires that attract the gaze of youth away from altruistic ventures and onto themselves. The obvious message is that the one with the most—and better—toys wins in the end. That person wins the girl or boy, wins the game, wins at life.

Prong Three: Youth as Rebellious

The groundwork was laid by G. Stanley Hall's tumultuous diagnosis, and since that time youth have been viewed as raging rivers out of sync with authority. A generation gap is assumed, and more than a few teens are heard to say, "I'm a teenager. I'm supposed to rebel!" Many adults hold this same belief, thus they tend to withdraw from adolescents during this time, rather than stay engaged with them. They assume the default mode of young people is to reject the codes and conventions of society, which leads to further intergenerational disconnect. Because of this assumption, teenagers are often blamed for things that aren't their responsibility. In terms of employment, for example, the tendency is to believe that the young person is at fault when he or she hasn't found a career by age 30, and that lack of stable work is an act of individual defiance, rather than an indication of diminishing workplace opportunities.

Prong Four: Youth as Only Peer-Oriented

Any movie that features teenagers portrays them as peer-oriented.[7] They're usually shown hanging out at the local corner, mall, or skate park with people just like them: rebellious, consuming, and self-absorbed. Further, it's suggested that teens want their space and that an adult's role is to withdraw. *After all,* the thinking goes, *youth is the time to "sow wild oats" and work out the kinks of adolescence. What adult wants to be around that? Young people want their freedom, and in the end it works out best for everyone if we just give it to them.* The message communicated to adults is, "They don't want to spend time with us" and "they aren't interested in adults." However, this "peer-oriented" logic masks a key reality of youth—specifically, the liability that is linked to adult absence during this crucial part of the life cycle.

An Antidote: A New Ideology of Youth

A consumer-driven agenda supported by a viral capitalism keeps youth in the orange crate with little room to grow beyond the ideological code. Across North American society, there are few signs of a concerted effort by adult institutions to deal with the troubles of young people. That means we'll continue to see internalized frustration—anxiety, depression, suicide, and substance abuse—as well as diverse signs of externalized frustration, such as cyberbullying and road rage.

However, in this environment James Côté and Anton Allahar remind us that socially produced behaviors can be socially *re*duced in plenty of ways.[8] Our proposal is that the church take up the challenge to seriously understand the sociological plight of teenagers and then offer a liberating new framework of youth and a renewed optimism for adulthood. This new ideology of youth can find expression inside the church through an intentionally lived vocation culture. Vocational imagination would encourage change in the understanding of who teenagers are called to be and what they're called to do in the world. It would involve churches, parachurch organizations, youth, and adults engaging in the work of understanding and arranging life around questions and practices of vocation. And the exciting news is that it's already happening in various ways and in diverse places. (Later on in this book, we'll introduce you to one real-life example of this involving a denomination, its churches, and its seminary.)

In *Becoming Adult, Becoming Christian*, James Fowler likens it to "the motion of dance, or the disciplined freedom of theatrical improvisation, or the responsive creativity of good conversation, in which the participants are really 'all there.'"[9] This implies that we'll all need to have a much more intentional role—to be really "all there."

Therefore, we suggest an antidote to the consumerist virus (that old consumerist, selfish, rebellious, age-segregated ideological code for youth) via a new imaginative ideology based on a biblically informed understanding of youth. This is a definition of youth that's squarely anchored in seeing teenagers not as problems to be solved but as people with capacity. This is a definition of youth that sees teenagers as people who have something to offer and something to contribute *now* (not only at some distant point in the future). This is a vision of youth that sees teenagers as having the capacity to see beyond themselves now and be fully capable of focusing on others and their needs.

Yes, we're suggesting an antidote, if you will, to the current consumerist code. What we offer next is a new way of seeing teenagers, a new code, or elements of a new story. There are four important components of this new "code," and while the explanation of each isn't nearly exhaustive, it's offered here as a starting point.

Youth as Called

Youth are called into being by a Creator. Out of nothing God has shaped teenagers in the world to be free, creative—and ultimately themselves. This happens when they simply are the unique creations they were designed to be. They are christened—a divine gift to the world—and made like none other. All the beauty and diversity that only a creative, omnipotent God could dream up was placed in their human shells.

Liberation then comes as youth hear and live these authentic selves. Parker Palmer, in his exuberant little book called *Let Your Life Speak: Listening for the Voice of Vocation*, reminds us that the concept of vocation flows from the Latin root *voice*. The secret to authentic living is listening. "Vocation does not mean a goal that I pursue. It means a calling that I hear," writes Palmer.[10] Vocation or calling, says James Fowler, is "the response a person makes with his or her total self to the address of God and to the calling of partnership."[11]

Notice that the emphasis revolves around a total response of the self, a listening, and a life theme . . . something deep within us. As youth learn to read their responses to their experiences, they learn that vocation "is a text we are writing unconsciously every day we spend on earth."[12] From this youth learn about living a life of depth and meaning, rather than living a life that is shallow and without purpose.

Youth as Others-Oriented

We were created to be a blessing to others and to God. It's something our authentic lives cannot help but be. However, there is a huge chasm between the self-serving ego and the authentic, others-oriented self. But let us be clear—you don't become others-oriented by either going with the flow or following the "shoulds" of those around you. Again, we turn to Palmer, who suggests "from our first days in school (or in front of television), we are taught to listen to everything and everyone but our (deepest) selves."[13] The torrent of media and marketing images and sounds provide us with guidance for how to live. But rarely do we truly acknowledge the deeper, spot on, genuine self that is a gift to the world.

When Mother Teresa was eighteen, she asked her mentoring priest how she could tell if God was calling her into some vocation. The answer she received was a wise one. Father Jambrenkovic said, "You can know it by the happiness you feel. . . . a deep joy is like the compass which points out the proper direction for your life. One should follow this even when one is venturing on a difficult path."[14] Her truest self led her to an orientation of being others-centered, and it was a path she followed for the rest of her life.

Youth as Resourced

God creates each person as unique. God also gives teenagers an undeniable disposition of delight that's oriented toward their neighbors. But God does more. He also empowers teens to live that calling. God desires nothing more than to give. The apostle Paul states that God began a good work in each of us, and he will complete it (Philippians 1:6). Quite literally and theologically, it is Christ doing the work—performing through the teenagers as they're energized by God. They can do far more than we give them credit for—especially given the reality that youth can, right now, live into their calling with practice. Practice is, of course, a concept most youth are used to—from sports to music to schoolwork and more.

It's a perspective and a language that's missing. Most youth just don't have the language of vocation and calling in their lives. They're more inclined to ask—or perhaps more to the point, others are asking for them—"Who am I becoming?" and "What am I to do?" instead of dealing with others-focused notions of vocation and calling such as "Who is God calling me to become?" and "Whom am I to serve?" Fred Edie, director of the Duke Youth Academy, suggests that "Christian youth find it nearly impossible to imagine the God of deep mystery calling *them* in the midst of their ordinary lives and inadequacies."[15] And while we agree, we also would nudge that just a bit further to suggest that often it's also the adults and the cultural climate that surround youth that just don't believe they have what it takes to accomplish something bigger than themselves. Instead, consumer culture breeds dependence and simply sells youth short with a competing vision for what their lives can be about.

Therefore, every youth needs to know that all the resources needed to live the life of a unique calling are available from God. This is empowering for teens and opens up new vistas and the eyes with which to see. Teenagers want to feel competent and to contribute something and to know this isn't done alone—that God is actually at work in them and through them. This knowledge not only is life-giving but also forges the path and encourages the move to adulthood.

Youth in Community

Lastly, youth are not alone. In fact Paul, in his impressive letter to the Ephesians, describes an organic community that is a body. Every part is supported by the others, all organically working together with Christ as the head in order to bring shalom to every corner of broken creation. This type of connectedness suggests that teenagers will find others who will joyfully support them in whatever ventures they're uniquely and deeply called to. They'll find mentorship and support as they try to figure out their vocations and live their faith. There will be a readiness and willingness to serve each other. They will find adults who include youth in the "adult world," helping them actually become a real part of it. They will find adults and a wider community that demonstrates an adult resilience—with adults coming back again and again in their efforts to connect with teens—in spite of teenagers' apparent disinterest. But in order for any of this to happen, youth must actually engage with adults—a community of adults, in fact.

Some kind of adolescence restructuring must happen—not so much through youth themselves but rather in the minds and effort of adults, because strong and deep connections between youth, adults, and the adult world determine not only how teens behave but who they become.

Currently most youth are without some essential fundamental nutrients—i.e., adult connections and adult rewards of autonomy, competence, and mastery—which spur growth toward adulthood. Therefore after adolescence there is . . . more adolescence. Societal changes have conspired against not only the innate desire of teens to move toward greater maturity but also against youth-adult connections, encouraging what's been called "the endless adolescence."[16]

Relationships Rediscovered

"Relationships are and remain central to all of human life," writes N. T. Wright, challenging us to rediscover relationships.[17] Wright suggests that time and time again it is the Christian community that is called upon to model new patterns of community life shaped by intimacy, friendship, mutual delight, admiration, and respect. "Be kind to one another, tenderhearted, forgiving each other, just as God in Christ also has forgiven you. Therefore be imitators of God, as beloved children; and walk in love, just as Christ also loved you and gave Himself up for us" (Ephesians 4:32–5:2 NASB). Growing up and maturing involves developing a disposition that leans heavily toward a positive kindness. As adults model this type of maturity, Wright suggests that not only are relationships rediscovered but also a greater work of restoration takes place. And this needs to be done in the company of teenagers.

Three things mark this work of restoration, this *shalom* of God on earth, and invite our participation from the societal level down to the individual level: restorative justice; healing, kind relationships; and beauty reborn in creation and the arts.[18] As we discern calling—and, with intention, shape a vocational culture in our midst and in our communities—we, in fact, are offering teenagers a liberating antidote to the infectiousness of a market-driven culture. When this new ideology of youth becomes infused with the imaginations of youth workers and consciously embraced by youth ministries, churches, and communities, the restraints of all lesser views of youth will most definitely fall away.

The Church as a Buffer

Christian Smith suggests that churches and youth ministries provide a buffer against a market that stimulates the ego gratification of advanced capitalism. In his landmark study of youth and religion in the United States, he found significant pro-social differences in adolescents who belonged to faith communities. Astonishingly there were many social zones where pro-social outcomes were positively correlated to participation in faith communities.

Participation by youth in faith communities is found to be:

1. Inversely related to juvenile drug, alcohol, and tobacco use, and to delinquency
2. Inversely related to thoughts of suicide, attempted suicide, and actual suicide, including being a protective influence against suicide among youth most at risk for it
3. Correlated with overall satisfaction with life, more involvement with families, and better skills in solving health-related problems
4. A factor fostering positive educational outcomes, including academic achievement from childhood through college and being a protective influence against dropping out of school for at-risk youth
5. Linked to commitment to and involvement in community service and greater political and civic involvement in young adulthood[19]

Why are these outcomes more prevalent among religious youth? Perhaps it's because an alternative vision of what could be is proving to be an antidote to the capitalist consumer virus. Smith's own conclusions hint at this. He says communities (of faith) promote specific directives of self-control, self-sacrifice, and personal virtue into which members are inducted, such that youth may internalize alternative moral orders and use them to guide their life choices. This acts as a buffer to the moral order of mass consumer market capitalism whose "virtues" include self-gratification, self-assertion, competition, insecurity, conformity, perpetual experimentation, contempt for traditional authorities, the commodification of all value, and incessant material acquisition.[20]

There are already many adults who "see" teenagers through a different lens. And there are many wide-ranging and life-giving youth ministries and parachurch organizations providing experiences for youth that encourage a new way of engaging life. But there are still far too many teens who are missing this vibrant understanding of their own purpose. We advocate that churches, parishes, and parachurch organizations courageously offer all young people within their sphere a new ideology of youth—rooted theologically—that engages an actively lived vocational culture.

In their own call for a new ideology of youth, James Côté and Anton Allahar point to Sweden, where the state has instituted a National Department of Youth Affairs with the following three focuses:

- Youth Independence: commitment to youth independence and the right to good education, good career, and good accommodation
- Youth Influence: genuine opportunity for youth influence and participation
- Youth Resource: youth commitment, creativity, and critical thinking are viewed as resources[21]

Slightly modified, we'd suggest that youth ministry strive to offer the following comparable destinations for all youth in their circle of influence to receive the following:

- Youth Independence: commitment to youth independence and the right to theological vocation, joyful service, and good accommodation within our faith community
- Youth Influence: genuine opportunity for youth influence and participation in the community at large
- Youth Resource: youth commitment, creativity, and critical thinking are viewed as resources

A church, parish, or parachurch group that continually blesses teenagers is also a place where both youth and adults are continually living out of vocation. In a culture that tells us that being a good consumer is what matters most, it's easy for the church to simply say that being good consumers of *church activities* is what matters. However, a church that calls out youth to discern their vocations and then empowers them to live out of their calling is also a place where youth can experience the hospitality to ask the big questions and dream worthy dreams. Furthermore, it's also very likely a place where a different ideological code is at work and where a different story is being written. It's a place where a new, robust countercultural ideology of youth is deeply rooted. Perhaps this is *your* youth ministry.

Discussion and Study Questions

1. How does a consumer-driven youth culture distort and diminish the lives of teenagers? In what ways does it distort the relationships adults have with teenagers? And how does a consumer culture distort what it means to be "adult"?

2. Adolescence has been defined as starting in puberty and ending with how a society or community defines *maturity*. How can faith communities contribute to defining *adulthood* and *maturity*? How would theological definitions of *adulthood* and *maturity* read (reflecting on these passages and verses as starting points: Proverbs 1:5; 1 Corinthians 13:4-8, 11; 14:20; Ephesians 4:11-14; 5:1-2; 1 Timothy 4:12; Hebrews 5:14; 6:1; 1 John 2:14)?

3. Take a few moments to think about the four prongs of the beginning ideology of youth from this chapter. What would you add? How would you make this ideology deeper and more robust?

4. In what tangible ways could youth ministry be shaped and informed by:

   - a commitment to youth independence, encouragement to be adults, and the application of a theologically informed vocation and identity for youth;
   - opportunities for youth influence and participation in which youth's creativity and growing critical thinking skills are seen as resources to the community.

   What would youth ministry look like if shaped by these commitments? In what ways would it differ from the present form?

Try this . . .

View this talk from designer and educator Kiran Bir Sethi (http://www.ted.com/talks/kiran_bir_sethi_teaches_kids_to_take_charge.html). One of Sethi's principal convictions is embedding education in real-world contexts, where the boundaries between "school" and "life" blur and learning becomes more of a journey for children (i.e., where they can see the change that's needed, be changed, and then lead the change). "It starts with believing in kids," she says. "When adults believe in children and say 'you can!' then they will." Compare and contrast Sethi's observations of and belief in children with what you presume that (or have heard firsthand from) typical adults regarding belief in children. Is there a difference? If so, to what do you attribute that difference? How might those beliefs about children eventually inform or shape the beliefs that adults would have about teenagers and what they are capable of?

REIMAGINING YOUTH MINISTRY

5

GROWING UP CONSUMED AND THE PLACE OF YOUTH MINISTRY

They are essentially consumers rather than producers. Their contacts with adults are likely to occur in highly controlled environments such as the classroom, and the adults encountered are usually conveyors of specialized services such as education and guidance.

—Joseph Kett[1]

What kids need from adults is not just rides, pizza, chaperones, and discipline. They need the telling of stories, the close ongoing contact so that they can learn and be accepted. If nobody is there to talk to, it is difficult to get the lessons of your own life so that you are adequately prepared to do the next thing. Without a link across the generations, kids will only hear the next thing.

—Patricia Hersch[2]

From the music of John Mayer to movies like *Garden State* to the experience of a quarter-life crisis, it's easy to tell that something is in the air. Youth workers can sense it. The teenagers you work with mostly look like teenagers. But the ground on which they stand has shifted, and many teens have become anxious and confused, choosing to soothe their anxiety by consuming. Many adolescents make it to adulthood and do it quite well. What's troubling, though, is that more and more youth seem to be having a difficult time getting there.

To the perceptive youth worker, the twentieth-century invention of the "teenager" and the life stage of "adolescence" is not news. Changes and growth in mass education, child-labor laws, urbanization, mass consumerism, the media, and their combined impact on youth, however, is becoming more newsworthy. What was once a practical, short transition to adulthood is now a more complex experience—one that can extend well into a person's late twenties. Teenagers face daily decisions fueled by unlimited and unfiltered information. Some decisions are benign, others lead to a lifetime of possibilities, and still others may carry a lifetime of responsibilities.

Novelist Nick Hornby, author of *About a Boy* and *High Fidelity*, captured a sense of this transition in a witty novel titled *Slam*. A boy named Sam narrates his own story about being raised by his young, divorced mother. Sam is an average teenager and a decent student who plans to be the first person in his family to attend and graduate from college. At fifteen, skateboarding is his passion, and his Tony Hawk poster was the "coolest present ever." (In the novel the poster serves as Sam's imaginary mentor—he talks to it and "Tony" responds.) Life moves along as "normal" as possible until Sam's girlfriend, Alicia, gets pregnant. Then Sam and Alicia must face some pretty major decisions.

Sam's story is all about making—and living with—decisions among the myriad things going on when one is fifteen years old. And Hornby's clever narrative style provides a glimpse into how teenagers are shaped by current youth culture and how they might process and wade through the dilemmas, decisions, and questions of the day. "One thing I can tell you," Sam says about what he learned from those couple of years of his story, "is this. Age isn't like a fixed thing. You can tell yourself that you're seventeen or fifteen or whatever, and that might be true, according to your birth certificate. But birth certificate truth is only a part of it. You slide around, in my experience. You can be seventeen and fifteen and nine and a hundred all on the same day."[3]

Hijacked Stories

In advanced industrialized societies, relentless consumer culture powerfully shapes the meaning and purpose of the story and experience of growing up. Consumer culture bends in ways to contain and channel youth as a commodity—a target market—and teenagers can experience this in much the same way as Sam describes as so much sliding around between feeling seventeen, nineteen, and nine all on the same day. Consumer culture reduces teenagers to the role of passive consumers, while at the same time it attempts to give meaning to "the story of youth" in the hope of repackaging it and selling it again, and again, and again.

Consider Jean Twenge's conclusions in *Generation Me*.[4] Written for a wide mainstream audience, the book explores some of the themes we've been looking at so far in this book and, more specifically, the effects that these packaged and repackaged stories are having in the lives of young adults. Twenge's observation is that youth are confident, tolerant, open-minded, and self-asserting yet cynical, depressed, lonely, and anxious. According to Twenge, our culture's mainstream institutions have taught teenagers to put their own needs first, encouraged them to believe that they can be whatever they want to be, and convinced them that life is all about consumption and gratification. Taking these messages to heart, Twenge notes the greater effect they've had on young adults. They find it difficult to adjust when "real life" turns out to be off-message. "But if you think about it," writes Donald Miller, "all our consumerism is hijacking our stories."[5] When real life bumps up against the mediated consumer story we live in and turns out to be off-script, it's unsettling at best. And at worst, it's jarring, gloomy, and demoralizing. Miller is right—growing up consumed results in hijacked stories.

Growing Up Consumed

Sit with any group of adults and it's likely that the conversation will turn to teenagers at some point. The next time you're in a situation like this, put yourself just outside of the conversation and listen for what's being said and how. Not too long ago, I overheard a rather animated conversation between a small group of adults sitting at the next table at Starbucks. By all appearances this little gathering seemed to consist of well-meaning, good-hearted, thoughtful, genuine parents. Furthermore it seemed that one parent's fifteen-year-old was "giving her some trouble." The nature of the trouble wasn't elaborated, but the responses of the other group members were telling: "Oh well. That's what fifteen-year-olds do—give their parents grief." To be sure, some fifteen-year-olds do give their parents grief, but on the whole, do *all* fifteen-year-olds do this? The person making that claim (with an authoritative tone that was most likely intended to soothe the anxious worries of a friend) seemed pretty sure that the role of fifteen-year-olds *was* in fact to make trouble for their parents.

It was just a passing comment made in a coffee shop—doesn't mean much, right? Oh, but it does. And if you were to think about it for a few minutes, you could probably come up with your own examples of similar "passing comments" that—in a small way—lift the curtain on what many adults believe to be true about teenagers. It has become a truism that adolescence not only is a difficult life stage but one riddled with inevitable troubles, with youth themselves "troubled" . . . and the *source of* trouble for adults around them. Driven by raging hormones and an immaturity that we are relatively helpless to change, it seems many adults believe this to be true of all adolescents. Yet, the thing is—sometimes we get what we expect.

What we're suggesting is that this is the power of a culture or society's unifying myth about teenagers. It's a story—an overarching, socially constructed narrative—that a society builds and tells itself in many different ways about teenagers. "But since everyone is immersed in this narrative and lives it, it is rarely laid out in a beginning-middle-end kind of story."[6] Our concern here is to wonder whether Christian adults ever stop to consider the way they imagine the world of youth. Given that we are immersed in the same culturally determined story, we see teenagers through many of the same lenses and often end up slotting them into a generalized story about what it means to be a teenager. What are the elements of that story, and where do they come from? How do we imagine what it means to be young? How do teenagers imagine themselves and their stories? What is the big story they're arranging their lives by? How might we positively influence that narrative and what is the place of youth ministry in that task?

Consumer Culture Shapes the Story

"Consumer capitalism," writes Rodney Clapp, "is much more pervasive, and much less obvious, than smog or billboards. Look harder, and you can see it at work all around: shaping attitudes, bending behaviors, grinding and refracting an endless series of lenses through which to see and experience the world in a particular way."[7] In her book *Brands of Faith*, Mara Einstein adds, "People, on average, will see close to 200 advertisements a day, but may see upwards of 3,000 marketing messages in the same time period through branded products, T-shirts, and product placement; that's almost 11 million branded messages per year."[8]

Ad-men Terry O'Reilly and Mike Tennant, in their book *The Age of Persuasion*, tell us that advertisers often ignore arguments and tangibles and instead go directly for creating an emotional impression. "A brand is more than an abstract idea, a slogan, or a logo. It's an experience that appeals to the senses and the emotions. John Wayne's brand is about being tough, honest, and durable but with a soft heart. Switzerland's brand is embodied in chocolate, precise timepieces, and pristine villages amid snow-capped mountains. Albert Einstein's brand is that of a gentle, disheveled, childlike genius. It doesn't matter whether or not these images are real because brands aren't about what you know; they're about what you feel."[9]

Believing that the "brand" is losing ground in the overgrown marketing landscape, Kevin Roberts, CEO Worldwide of Saatchi & Saatchi, a major marketing company, now speaks of the future beyond brands in terms of "Lovemarks."[10] According to the Saatchi & Saatchi website, "a Lovemark is a product, service or entity that inspires loyalty beyond reason."[11] In other words, Lovemarks are the evolution of a brand. It's all about how the meaning of a product is shaped and how the consumer's attitude toward a product is experienced and felt, not the benefits of using the product itself.

A Lovemark attains high levels of respect when it delivers beyond the expectation of great performance. This is no different than what good brands do. But according to Roberts, Lovemarks will transcend regular brands when they touch your heart as well as your mind. This is the evolution of the love angle. It's about creating a deep personal and emotional connection between a product or service and the consumer. Remember, we're essentially talking about a concept designed to sell stuff.

The really interesting thing to notice is the language Roberts uses to describe the character of Lovemarks. They're a blend of the following ingredients:

- Mystery—great stories; tap into dreams, myths, and icons; inspiration

- Sensuality—the five senses: sound, sight, smell, touch, and taste
- Intimacy—passion, commitment, empathy[12]

It's no wonder, then, that savvy brand leaders have discovered they're selling something far more than just a product.

What is the extent of this type of marketing? When Clapp asked historian Lendol Calder when he first noticed "the depth and width of consumerism in our culture," Calder recalled an experience from his college years at a Christian camp with people from several nations in attendance. A get-acquainted mixer had the college students divide into groups based on their nationalities, come up with a song that was representative of their culture, and then sing their chosen song for the larger group. Most of the groups had agreed on a song (typically a cultural folk song), practiced it, and were ready to perform after about twenty minutes. But the American students apparently debated which song they should sing for more than an hour. The names of rock songs, country songs, and others were tossed about, but there was no consensus among the group. When they finally settled on something to sing, it wasn't even a traditional song—it was a commercial jingle. They chose Coca-Cola's "I'd Like to Teach the World to Sing." At that moment Calder "realized that commercial culture was what finally and ultimately bound these Americans—these American *Christians*—together."[13]

Consumer Culture Shapes the Adolescent Story

The viral consumerist narrative is much more than a soft drink jingle. Essentially it's a story that says identity and fulfillment come through consumption and the collection of stuff. You are what you consume, the story goes. Identity becomes anchored externally to what you buy, what you can put on display, what you wear, and what you are associated with.[14] It's a "branded" identity, and what makes this branding even more confusing is that it isn't confined to a single market. Alissa Quart makes this point quite well in *Branded*, "While the mother strives to look twelve years younger, the daughter strives to look twelve years older. They meet in between."[15]

According to Wendy Murray Zoba, author of *Generation 2K*, mom and daughter meet in between because branding will always lead to a focus on self: "Our senses have grown dull and the consumer mindset has convinced us that *our* narrative is all that matters in the grand scheme of things. We like to think that 'the story' is ours to write, and we attempt to advance the plot according to what we think we deserve."[16] The only story that matters, then, is *my* story—and this creates part of the greater problem: that teenagers (and adults) find it very hard to turn themselves off in order to hear a different story.

Consider a couple of typical adolescent questions swirling about in the story: "Where do I fit?" and "Do I matter?" A consumer narrative quite readily suggests the answers and even provides the products to support them. But in doing so, it attempts to connect identity to the need to belong. The urge to belong can find a home in this narrative, uniting youth by what they're being sold—the brand, the image, the style, the story. As Alissa Quart explains, "Teenagers have come to feel that consumer goods are their friends—and that the companies selling products to them are trusted allies."[17] They've been branded. After all, these various brands solicit the opinions of teenagers with all the attentiveness of the perfect parent. And the brand is subsequently rewarded with young people's loyalty. With huge amounts of disposable income and their never-ending search for a story to believe in, youth are more than ready to hand over their bucks and their loyalty—and most do.

This is not to say that all youth are mindlessly obedient to the brand— far from it. For there will always be thoughtful and critical teenagers who are learning to live by some kind of counter-narrative and in awareness of the strategies of a mediated consumer culture. In fact, the good news is that more and more youth are having this conversation more often and in more and different kinds of places, from the school hallways to the church basement.

But in general terms, the majority of youth have been swayed by the appeal of the brand and what it promises. And it's easy to understand why. The consumer narrative sends very on-message signals that teenagers matter. However, it's akin to looking through darkly tinted glass— you can *almost* see what's on the other side of it. Teenagers *do* matter in the consumer story but not for any holistic reason. They matter only to the degree that they spend. They matter precisely because they *can* spend.

Previously, we introduced the business of cool hunters—the finders and communicators of image, style, and all things cool.[18] The cool-hunting process creates a feedback loop in which consumerism captures the trends, the image, and the style of cool from teenagers. Next, it packages what's cool, takes it to market, and sells it back to youth. Then teenagers consume and project it back. In fact, they're just taking on the cool that they'd already embraced.

The story of what it means to grow up is shaped and informed by a culture of consumption. And the message to teenagers is clear: image and style matter, and the opposite of that doesn't matter much at all. Consumerism has become, to echo Rodney Clapp's words, the lens through which teenagers see and experience the world, and they continue to imitate that which they see. Thus, the cool-hunting process repeats itself because the shelf life of "cool" continues to get shorter and shorter. Once something cool has been made available to the masses, it loses its cache. So cool moves on to the next thing. But the more efficient the feedback loop, the harder it becomes to locate cool.

The viral spread of the ideological code reinforces the beliefs of a consumer-focused story. Over time and in subtle ways, the needs of youth are bent for another purpose. Whether it's questions of identity (you are what you buy) or the need to belong (branding), these struggles are being shaped by this story. The code bends and shapes the story even more, so that it actually alters what we believe about teenagers (i.e., that they are rebellious, consuming, and self-absorbed). Teenagers are growing up consumed—and by a story that's not their own.

Why Consumer Culture Can Shape the Adolescent Story

In his book *Identity: Youth and Crisis*, Erik Erikson developed an early theory of identity formation. Involved in developing identity, he said, was the idea of choosing a system of meaning or an "ideology that has compelling power."[19] He also wrote that identity and ideology are both part of the same maturing process. Erikson's notion of adolescence also focused on the idea of "moratorium"—that socially acceptable "time-out" period during which teenagers are given the time and space to figure out who they are and what holds that "compelling power" for them. So the question becomes, "Who will shape identity? And what compelling and powerful ideas will capture our youth's attention during what's become a 'time-out' period that's even longer than it was during the time when Erikson was writing?" It's a question about meaning and who will provide it. This is also the time when questions of vocation start taking on significance. And although these questions take on a laser-like focus in young adulthood, adolescence is the time when they get placed "on the table" of life.

Kenda Creasy Dean has written convincingly in *Practicing Passion: Youth and the Quest for a Passionate Church* that we must understand that times have changed significantly from the time when Erikson was writing, mainly during the 1950s and 1960s. The problem with choosing an identity or ideology—or even addressing questions of vocation—during adolescence is that it involves teenagers learning to trust themselves and others, as well as a readiness and ability to be faithful to what they choose. This ability is what Erikson termed "fidelity," a disciplined devotion that enables us to be there—to be present—for another person. And here's the thing Dean wants us to notice: this ability to be "for" another person is learned by experiencing someone being "for" us (that sense of having someone in your corner). "In short, fidelity cannot be achieved; it can only be received from those who practice it on our behalf."[20] Erikson called those people "affirming companions," adults who not only embody worthy ideologies and stories to live by, but also truly see and notice teenagers and respond to their desires to be seen and noticed.[21]

Dean also wants us to notice that at the time that Erikson was writing, he assumed the presence of faithful adults to be a commonplace reality in the lives of teenagers. Michael Warren writes in *Awakening Youth Discipleship*, "For Erikson identity is an active synthesis of a person's essence as worked out in community."[22] What we've come to realize is that this would be an optimistic assumption in our current youth culture. Whether it's "a tribe apart" or the "world beneath," we have an increasing sense that today's teenagers have few adults and even fewer institutions that are prepared to be there for them.[23] And so it's in the "tribe" or in that "world beneath" that youth operate in an almost default society while attempting to help each other grow up. "In short," Dean writes, "Erikson's theory of identity formation relied on an ingredient no longer widely available to North American young people: grown-ups."[24]

In his essay "The Imaginations of Youth," Michael Warren takes Erikson a step further and suggests that we also pay attention to Charles Taylor's concept of the self as it's set out in his *Sources of the Self: The Making of the Modern Identity*.[25] It's also suggested that the deeply felt question of "Who am I?" is present not only during the teenage years. On the contrary, it doesn't go away, and it's revisited again and again. Identity is defined by the commitments and identifications that provide a frame of reference or the "horizon" out of which persons are able to make a stand. To not have this "horizon" or orientation about where one stands and for what (a disorientation and uncertainty) is to not know who one is (an identity crisis). Settling on and renegotiating commitments and identifi-cations (where one stands and what one stands for) is very much a com-munal activity—it can't be done alone. And for many youth, there is no social or communal chorus of adults providing a validating voice about direction, commitments, and identifications. Instead, there is a void.

Into the void enters the virus: the consumer capitalist virus that leaves its code and bends the story. Participation in the consuming story requires only money (which teenagers have), not maturity (which teen-agers are still developing). Teens are ready to receive a different story and are looking for adult "guarantors" to walk with them; but they don't often find such "affirming companions" who are up for the task. It is into this space—in this part of the story—that faith communities, youth ministries, and parachurch groups can play a major and distinctive role. It is in these places where a new ideology of youth can be deeply rooted to shape a more compelling story of what it means to be a teenager. A new level of "walking with" can emerge between youth, adults, and entire congregations of adults encouraging young people to choose an ideology of compelling power, vocational purpose, and a big enough God—together.

Consuming Youth and the Place of Youth Ministry

In *The Magician's Nephew,* C. S. Lewis tells the story of how Aslan created Narnia—in essence, it's the "beginning of the story." Toward the end of the book, Lewis takes a step back from the narrative account and tries to explain why Uncle Andrew and his nephew Digory see the world so differently. Andrew wants to withdraw from it, seeing it as a whole lot of noise, confusion, and chaos. Digory, on the other hand, is captivated by it. He's drawn to it more and more and sees it as a fascinating place full of wonder. Lewis then remarks, "For what you see and hear depends a good deal on where you are standing; it also depends on what sort of person you are."[26]

What you see and hear depends on where you're standing. The first part of *Consuming Youth* was designed to stand us in a different place. From that vantage point, it is our hope that we'll see the world of youth just a little differently now, putting us in a place where we can begin to see—and even hear—how and why most teenagers believe and respond in certain ways. From that vantage point, we hope you will recognize the viral parts of the youth narrative upon which many youth build their stories. Namely, that their identity and fulfillment come through consumption, that community can be experienced by buying into a brand's story, and that their independence can be gained by spending.

It also depends on what sort of person you are. In the face of consumerism's pervasive influence, we can offer a contrasting story. Ultimately, that's the whole point of Part Two of this book—to encourage you, in your own context, to find ways to cultivate and support a compelling contrasting story. Youth workers and other concerned adults who invest in teenagers' lives are people of energy and passion. You are people called to and called by a deeper, more compelling story—a story guided by compassion, hospitality, generosity, and service. Yours is a story of mission and a story of vocation. Within your story beats the impulse to invite youth to participate in and engage with this life-giving and contrasting story. And the implications of this impulse are far-reaching. They extend well beyond the lives of your youth to include a reimagining of the way we do church, youth ministry, and even the activity of parachurch organizations. In youth ministry you have an opportunity to reframe the story with a new ideological code, to extend community, and to confirm mission for this generation of teenagers.

To get there, we will quickly travel through the story of youth ministry as it has matured in practice. The intention is to relate enough of the youth ministry story so that we can begin to ask how the rise of a culturally accepted version of adolescence and the concurrent growth of a consumer-driven market economy have impacted both the shape of youth ministry and the response of the church to adolescence. This is, after all, a part of your story, too. As a youth worker—even if you consider yourself the adult on the fringes of youth work—these formative movements have shaped the ministry you do today.

Along the way we hope you'll look for and gain a little insight into the subtle ways youth ministry has been both shaped and affected by the expansion of adolescence and its relationship to consumer culture. "When you market spirituality," writes Mara Einstein, "you introduce people to the idea that they can shop for it, and so they will, or at least are more likely to."[27]

If teenagers are increasingly prone to shop (even shopping around for youth groups), will youth ministries have to increase their level of promotion in order to be heard in the mix of so much consumer noise? (Or have we already?) Do youth ministries feel subtle pressure to create a product—a better youth program—that religious consumers will "buy"? Just how has the church and youth ministry responded to the birth of adolescence and consumer culture?

Discussion and Study Questions

1. How does marketing affect you? How does it affect your desire for consumer goods? How does it affect your sense of happiness? How do you suppose marketing affects teenagers' sense of acceptance by their peers (e.g., whether they believe one is "in" or "out," cool or not)? Is marketing and the media that drives it just a mirror to culture—or something more? (For more on the calculated nature of marketing, we recommend the PBS Frontline documentary "The Persuaders" at http://www.pbs.org/wgbh/pages/frontline/shows/persuaders.)

2. What is your first memory of brand consciousness? How old were you? What was it? What did that brand offer you? How do you suppose a brand offers identity and individual vision to teenagers?

3. When identity is constructed in the flow of consumption, it can often feel as though there's little to hold on to, making identity much more fluid than it was in the past. How do you see this dynamic in your context? What issues does this raise for your youth, for you, and for your ministry? In what ways have the personae, self-images, ambitions, and values of young people in North America been distorted by the commercial frenzy surrounding them? How are young people affected by the marketing directed toward them? What are some specific symptoms of this distortion?

4. "In a commodity culture," observes Sky Jethani in *The Divine Commodity* (Zondervan, 2009, 37), "we have been conditioned to believe that nothing carries intrinsic value. Instead, value is found only in a thing's usefulness to us, and tragically this belief has been applied to people as well." A consumer culture eventually reduces everything to a commodity, objects of exchange, and

lives that focus on having rather than being. How have teens been reduced to commodities? How has that shaped and informed what we've come to believe about what being a teenager is all about? And how does this belief show up in real interactions with teenagers (among themselves and with adults)? How would we know if teens are internalizing the narratives shaped and mediated by our consumer-driven and media-saturated culture? In what ways has youth ministry itself become a commodity?

Try this . . .

With the proliferation of social-media technologies, advertisers are finding more avenues to target teenagers. With the Internet came pop-up ads, ads that run before video clips and games, ads that masquerade as contests, and sponsored Google links that match your search terms. But as technology advances, and youth gravitate toward more social-media places and digital devices, so do advertisers. Even tweets from reality-TV stars and other celebrities can earn advertisers (and themselves) extra dollars if the tweets are about how much they like certain products. So research and document other ways advertisers sneak into the wired and socially networked world of youth and discuss what effects these stealth marketing methods might have on youth.

6

RADIOS AND RALLIES: YOUTH MOVEMENTS RESPOND TO ADOLESCENCE

There are very few things today done in youth work that were not pioneered in Youth for Christ or Young Life—be it in Christian camping, various small group activities or music.

—Attributed to Dr. Jay Kesler[1]

But it's critical to remember that—as easy as it is to critique from our perspective—these youth workers were revolutionaries.

—Mark Oestreicher[2]

To this point we have briefly traced the rise of adolescence and the concurrent rise of the market economy. The line between the two, if there was any, became significantly blurred with the rise of consumerism. The work of a market economy is to sustain the exchange between product and consumer; they're sold to us, and we consume. What we are slow to notice in that exchange is how consumerism distorts and diminishes our lives and the lives of teenagers. It also has the potential to distort and diminish the ways in which the church responds to adolescence.

Youth ministry was on the rise at the same time adolescence was emerging both as a force and as a target market. With any endeavor there are always unintended outcomes, and this is true when we consider the church's response to the rise of adolescence. Has our approach to youth and youth ministry been shaped more by the prevailing belief about adolescence and the consumer-shaped youth culture?

In a Facebook discussion about the book *Youth Ministry 3.0*, Professor Darwin Glassford asked the question this way: "I am left with a nagging sense that no matter how well we understand the life issues and culture, we will still be frustrated. I wonder what would happen if we abandoned the social construct of adolescence in our churches and ministries and saw young people as young adults who are to be mentored into adult roles and responsibilities?"[3]

One Size Doesn't Fit

The band was absurdly talented. Although the doors to the massive auditorium were closed, the sound was pristine, and the student band was playing a tune by Genesis so well that even the band's biggest fans would have been fooled. We were ushered inside before the students, and we observed the precision with which staff and volunteers completed a pre-event checklist. A glitch emerged as the large screen that was to rise from the stage didn't do what it was supposed to do. And with executive panache, the decision was made—in the moment—not to show the video that was to appear on that screen. The countdown continued.

We were taken up to the balcony seats that were being held for us. And then with sound and lights that could rival any good rock 'n' roll show, the doors were opened and waves of students, hundreds of them, rushed to the areas where their team banners were displayed. From the vantage point of our balcony seats, we were watching and learning. This was the late '80s and youth ministry had certainly caught on and seemed to be hitting its stride . . . sort of.

Taken as a whole, what that particular ministry was doing with and for students was nothing short of spectacular. At least that's how it looked to us. And to be fair, there's no question that good youth ministry was indeed happening. During a question-and-answer period following the event, the youth pastor was quick to point out areas of weakness as well as strength. It was fairly easy to spot the problems, the holes if you will, in the strategy. Yet a deeper dilemma was at work—one that was barely recognized and not given much floor time. From our vantage point in the balcony, it appeared that all of those seminars and ministry-specific, first-person accounts began to take root in a copy-and-paste or one-size-fits-all way of thinking.

One-size-fits-all thinking has always been an Achilles heel in ministry—and youth ministry is no exception. Take, for example, the "Akron Plan" in church architecture.[4] First used in Akron, Ohio, back in the early days of the Sunday school movement, this building design featured a vast, open, theater-like space with a "superintendent's" desk featured on a high stage and classroom spaces sectioned off around the edges of the auditorium. The design was considered the best form for any Sunday school using uniform lessons. The superintendent could lead the opening exercises, keep an eye on the classes, and review the morning's lesson at the close—all from the desk perched high on the stage. "By 1910 most 'new' Sunday school buildings had encased the outmoded uniform lesson plan in expensive brick and mortar."[5]

The problem with such thinking is that we uncritically adopt approaches to ministry that further marginalize youth and uncritically buy in to marketplace consumer versions of adolescence. There is an eagerness to apply pre-packaged programs because they appear to work. One-size-fits-all thinking has been problematic as far back as those initial days of the early youth movements.

Early Youth Movements[6]

"Pinpointing the genesis of youth ministry," writes Mark Cannister, "is not as simple as one might imagine."[7] He has a point. Some histories begin with Robert Raikes (1780), a newspaper publisher from Gloucester, England, and the growth of the Sunday school movement in Great Britain, sometime around the start of the Industrial Revolution. With the Industrial Revolution underway and its effects slowly being felt, Raikes' concern was the growing numbers of urban poor and providing literacy training for the children and youth who worked in the factories six days a week and then wandered about unsupervised and causing damage on the outlying countryside on Sundays.[8]

"Adolescence" hadn't been socially constructed at this point, so it would be stretching the idea to pinpoint this as the beginning of youth ministry. But we do see the seedlings of what will emerge as one of the building blocks of youth ministry: to protect youth from the evils of society, as seen in Raikes' preoccupation with wanting to "shape preventative measures against juvenile delinquency."[9] With the formation of the American Sunday School Union in 1824, the idea of Sunday school took root in North America and then it grew. By the 1840s, however, there were signs that the movement was starting to sputter and stall, and its influence began to bear the weight of denominational fractions.

A socially constructed perception of "adolescence" was still just on the horizon, but a vacuum was forming where once there were strong initiatives for youth. With the growth of industry came the movement of youth into the cities. So again from Great Britain, there came a response that eventually spread to the United States and Canada: the YMCA (Young Men's Christian Association) was founded in 1844, and its female counterpart, the YWCA, began in 1855.[10] The purpose of these two organizations was to help Christian young people maintain their Christian commitments after moving to the big city. They did this by providing them with a room, an introduction to good friends, and a place to read and relax and be trained as Sunday school teachers. Of course, as the agencies grew and matured, so did their purpose. But this was their initial thrust. What we see emerging in some of these early movements— just prior to the full-on invention of "adolescence"—are protectionist ideas that will, albeit in subtle ways, inform youth ministry years later.

The late 1800s were being shaped by civil conflicts, as well as growing cities. The age of onset of puberty was dropping, and the age of marriage was increasing. As these changes collided with the growth of publicly funded high schools, the results helped shape and structure a socially constructed adolescence. Factories sprung up, mass production fueled the beginning of mass marketing to inform consumers about this or that new invention—and then convince them that their lives would be better if they used it, which led to mass consumption. However, these same forces were pushing in on the YM/YWCA and weakening its position, making the time ripe for something a little different. According to David F. White in *Awakening Youth Discipleship*, what was to happen next "could not have emerged a century earlier and only gained momentum from the displacement of youth from other social roles."[11]

Into these pressure points stepped Francis E. Clark, pastor of Williston Congregational Church in Portland, Maine. In 1881, Clark had been looking for a way to support the young people of his church to continue growing in their faith. This was a simple and legitimate goal with a faint echo of the ideals of the earlier YMCA movement—but with a twist. Clark's Society of Christian Endeavor was open to youth aged thirteen to thirty and was divided into two groups: active and associate. The idea was essentially accountability—to assist youth in their desire to grow in their Christian endeavor. That took the form of a pledge and two commitments: (1) To be present at every Sunday evening meeting (unless absolute necessity prohibited it), and (2) Once a month share about the growth in your Christian experience over the past month. If a young person failed to keep these commitments, he would be removed from "active" status in the society.

Even though Endeavor was established for church youth, Clark made provision for an "associate" membership, seen as a first step toward an active Christian life.[12] And with this recognition of an associate membership, we have the beginning of a nuanced evangelistic thrust in Clark's Endeavor informed by a relational and testimonial contour. The Society was open to others, but it didn't actively seek them out. (This evangelistic impulse would find greater strength and prominence in the Youth for Christ movement just years ahead.)

As Clark's ideas spread, new "societies" were established and Christian Endeavor became popularized through articles, books, and eventually conventions. It was structured by area and regions, attracting those who wanted biblical grounding (the pledge) and those who wanted to be part of something larger and connected (regional meetings and conventions). From its beginning in 1881 and on into the 1920s and 1930s, Christian Endeavor grew and became one of the strongest and largest youth movements of its time. And like the forerunners of the Sunday school and the YMCA and YWCA, it still exists today, albeit with an updated and contemporized purpose.

Denominational groups couldn't help but notice that something was happening, and many felt that Clark's Christian Endeavor might provide the needed spark to reignite their youth societies. And so, armed with books and conventions, they began to shape and inform their denominational youth societies with the Endeavor pledge and principles. Not being fully satisfied with Endeavor, some denominations eventually organized their own youth organizations: the Epworth League (Methodist), the Walther League and the Luther League (Lutheran), Westminster Fellowship and Presbyterian Youth Fellowship (Presbyterian), Reformed Church Youth Fellowship, Nazarene Youth Fellowship, Baptist Youth

Fellowship, and the Baptist Young People's Union (Southern Baptist) to name a few.

With the issues of the day pressing on denominations and churches, denominational leaders added to the original Christian Endeavor structure, broadening their focus to include teaching on denominational loyalty (keeping young people in the church) and leadership development. Despite being credible objectives, they stretched and pulled at the structure in ways it wasn't designed for, and the overall effort was weakened. Yet denominational youth societies carried on and became increasingly concerned about doing things to keep their youth in the church and out of the world.[13]

And with the rise of the high school, keeping youth in the church was proving to be difficult. Mainline denominational youth work pressed on into the 1960s until church leaders became concerned about the isolationist tendencies within youth work and cautioned that youth should be integrated into the whole church. Youth ministry programs and budgets were cut at the denominational levels with nothing left in their place to encourage or aid churches with the integration of youth into churches. Thus began the difficult days for mainline denominational youth ministry.[14]

Developments were afoot that would direct the ebb and flow of youth movements. One was the rise of the high school; another was happening just as G. Stanley Hall's *Adolescence* was being published in America. In 1904, Fred and Arthur Wood set out across Britain to "preach the gospel." And by 1911, they'd begun focusing their work on the youth—or "young life," as they'd say—formalizing in that same year as the "Young Life Campaigns." Their vision of a national movement of Christian youth winning their own generation to Christ and of young people serving in positions of leadership began to take shape. And like the youth movements before them, it was to catch on and capture a broader audience.

Radios and Rallies

With adolescence now being talked about as a sociological construct and many of Hall's ideas from *Adolescence* being embraced, additional outside influences combined to solidify adolescence as a social construction. The Great Depression, another world war, and the establishment of a universal high school education shook the landscape. Culturally, the advent of movies had overtaken vaudeville as the most popular form of entertainment, and advertising dollars in magazines was doubling—reaching well into the millions. The styles of youth and the fashions of the day were being noticed, copied, and marketed.

And then there was the high school. When you put more and more youth into one location at around the same time that movies, big bands, radio, phonographs, dime store novels, soda fountains, school athletics, cheerleaders, and school dances became the rage—you have all the ingredients you need for a youth culture. And into this setting emerged the Youth for Christ movement and a brand of youth ministry that made evangelism over edification a key thrust.

Lloyd Bryant had a vision of reaching the young people who had no relationship to a church or little in the way of religious connection. A key part of that vision was student leadership—young people themselves participating in the work of evangelistic efforts. Using just about any vehicle to get the gospel heard, Bryant engaged popular speakers for evangelistic rallies, open air meetings, conferences and retreats, but the vehicle that eventually brought focus to all his efforts was the youth center.

By 1936 he had developed 14 youth centers in the East which grew to about 40 not long after and an association to guide them. These youth centers became the center of evangelistic meetings which were held during the week thus offering a place for youth to gather and providing a social outlet for youth in the years following the Depression. Bryant then began pairing radio with the meetings eventually broadcasting them live.[15]

But it was a young man from Manitoba, Canada, who took radio (and its technology) and became "the heart and soul of the 20th century youth ministry movements."[16] When Percy Bartimus Crawford— economically deprived and with an abusive father—was a teenager, he left small-town Manitoba to seek his fortune in Southern California. What he discovered was the spiritual dimension to his life, and by 1931 he'd made his way through Biola, UCLA, Wheaton College, and finally Westminster Seminary in Philadelphia. Described as the master of the seven-minute sermon, his *Young People's Church of the Air* was broadcasting on a network of more than 275 radio stations. The rapid pace of his radio sermons and the growing popularity of variety shows soon influenced the nature of the large gatherings that were to become known as Youth for Christ evangelistic rallies. Percy used the pop culture music of the day in his broadcasts, and his message was as robust as the music. He spoke in a style and language that was very accessible to adolescents. Thus, the response to his evangelistic appeals soon turned into credibility for a new way to do youth ministry, and his staccato speaking style became the standard for which many young speakers would strive.

"Teenage" Arrives

Jon Savage makes the observation in *Teenage: The Creation of a Youth Culture* that by the late 1930s, with the increasing percentage of youth remaining in high school, a new market was opening up and opening big.[17] The adolescent was now targeted as a consumer, and the potential market was expanding by both age and class. By 1940, there were twice the number of youth in high school as there had been in 1930, and G. Stanley Hall's notion of adolescence had arrived as a force—and not for production but consumption. Increasingly what mattered was what youth could buy because of what those things said about who they were. With their purchasing power, a new "class" was emerging—the teenager.

Percy Crawford noticed these changes. He paved the way for future youth ministries by using "swing" music (the language of youth at the time), the media (radio, television, and publishing), camping (he founded Pinebrook Bible Camp), and even higher education (he founded The King's College, now located in New York City). Celebrity was becoming an important part of the teenage fabric. Magazines, movies, and certainly music were making teenagers ogle and swoon over crooners. Celebrities and athletes were becoming fixtures on the platforms at the large rallies, and musical talent was fashioned after the hit groups of the day. Among the many people influenced by Crawford was Jack Wyrtzen, who would build on the road paved by Crawford.

Gil Dodds, an athletic star (world-class miler) who frequently gave his testimony at Wyrtzen's rallies, observed: "Without Wyrtzen there would have been no Youth for Christ movement, as it was known in the mid-forties."[18] Wyrtzen's boldest moves were Saturday night rallies in New York City's Times Square, broadcasting them over one of the most powerful independent radio stations of the time. Within months thousands attended his "Word of Life" evangelistic rallies at major auditoriums in New York and elsewhere—events that other youth workers soon imitated. And like Crawford before him, Wyrtzen found land for a summer conference and camp center, which soon became "Word of Life Island"—and camp ministry would become his focus.

The ground on which youth ministry stood was shifting, and on to it stepped Jim Rayburn and the Young Life Campaign. While Rayburn pioneered a more conversational approach to speaking (his initial involvements were with mass rallies), by the mid '40s he was moving in new directions away from the radios and rallies. Like Crawford before him, Rayburn could anticipate and appreciate the changes that were shaking the ground with the new emerging youth culture.

Youth Movements and Adolescence

Cultural forces are always at work, and the early youth movements were attempts, at times, to counter those forces (and work with them) as best they could. Adolescence as a distinct stage of life was embedded in the cultural consciousness, and the theory first penned by Hall was now fully embraced by educators, pastors and clergy, parents, lawmakers, health care workers, and others. Not that everyone agreed with the Darwinian-influenced and fear-inducing ideas Hall spoke of, but they resonated with the times and provided the basis of a theory for their efforts.

The era of radios and rallies saw the early emergence of both church-based youth ministries and parachurch clubs that would make their presence felt in various ways—even up to today. In the church there was a slowly growing gap developing between the youth ministry and other programs of the church, such as Sunday school, that would continue to grow. The church had to deal with the emerging creation of adolescence and, according to Joseph Kett in *Rites of Passage*, the church had a hand in the invention. Kett argues that church youth organizations (including the soon-to-be formalized parachurch clubs), along with other holding agencies (colleges and high schools), created a self-contained world in which immaturity could not only be tolerated, but sustained, thus producing what Kett would suggest were "hollow youth."[19] This self-contained world would encompass more time in the years ahead, and in the church it would develop into a parallel youth culture as adolescence morphed from being merely a life stage to a consumer demographic as well.

Churches began responding to adolescence by hiring former parachurch workers who'd bring their relational instincts into the church.

While having an ear to the ground, youth ministry would listen to popular culture—from its music to the humor of the early days of *Saturday Night Live*—and would continue to forge new ways of reaching youth with media, sound, and lights.

As we turn to that part of the story, a question emerges: *Well-intentioned though we were, were we merely perpetuating that self-contained world in which both a socially constructed reality of adolescence and the marketplace consumer version were allowed to take root and shape our responses to teenagers?*

Discussion and Study Questions

1. What difference does it make for the practice of youth ministry today to know a history of youth ministry over the last 100 years?

2. As the story of youth ministry has unfolded over the years, we can see that it's fluctuated between a concern for evangelism and a concern for Christian nurture. What's your starting point for your own understanding of the purpose of youth ministry in relation to these two concerns? Has it changed over time? If so, what stimulated your change in thinking? If it hasn't changed, what is the strength of your position?

3. What in your view was the most interesting or important development of the early youth ministry movements? What can we learn from it?

4. In what ways can a consumer-driven culture distort and diminish the ways in which the church responds to adolescence? In what ways historically has our approach to youth and youth ministry been shaped by popular beliefs about adolescence and the consumer-shaped youth culture?

Try this . . .

Develop a timeline for the youth ministry you're either serving now or are most familiar with. The line represents the total life and history of the youth ministry in that setting. Mark the line by decades (this may be a shorter line for newer churches and organizations and, in many other cases, a much longer line representing many decades). Talk to individuals who would have been around during various decades so that most, if not all, of the timeline is covered. Ask them to recall events covering that period. Who were significant people and youth workers? Who were the pastors? What were the high and low points in the life of that congregation (that also impacted the youth ministry)? Were there any significant turning points in the youth ministry? How did the practice and commitments of the youth ministry change? What was happening in the wider culture at the time, and how did it influence, inform, or shape the youth ministry?

7

CLUBS AND CONNECTIONS: YOUTH MINISTRY CULTURE IN A BRANDED AGE

The world is changed. I feel it in the water. I feel it in the earth. I smell it in the air. Much that once was is lost, for none now live who remember it.

—Galadriel, speaking of Middle-earth, in the 2002 film
The Lord of the Rings: The Fellowship of the Ring

The future would be Teenage.[1]

—Jon Savage

Like the inhabitants of Middle-earth, many of those who spend time with young people have a growing sense that both the world they've known and the world of teenagers is changing. It's a sense of knowing that much remains the same, yet nothing remains the same. The coming-of-age map is being redrawn. After the Second World War, the demands of the expanding youth culture merged with the social policies of the day, giving adolescents some sense of growing freedoms. "The many possible interpretations of youth had been boiled down to just one: the adolescent consumer."[2] The future, concluded Jon Savage, would be teenage.

The four main characters of George Lucas's film *American Graffiti* (1973) meet at Mel's Drive-In to spend their last night of summer together. The film captures what being a teenager in 1962 was all about. The cruising, the fads, the slang, the hoods, sock hops, slow dancing, burgers—and all set to an early rock 'n' roll rhythm with the quintessential disc jockey, Wolfman Jack.

On that last night, we meet Steve (Ron Howard), the clean-cut, good-guy class president who plans to leave behind his girlfriend, Laurie (Cindy Williams), as he heads off for college the next day. Curt (Richard Dreyfuss), Laurie's older brother and friend to Steve, is the "brain" of the group. He's supposed to leave with Steve for college, but he's having major doubts about leaving behind a life that's good, safe, and predictable for the unknown that college holds. Terry (Charlie Martin Smith), the younger, more naive, and sort of nerdy guy of the group, gets guardianship of Steve's '58 Chevy. John Milner (Paul Le Mat) is a high school dropout and street-racing local legend who watches yet another group of grads move on without him.

Throughout the night each of these characters encounters a range of situations from carhops to sock hops, from street racing to car crashes, from the burger place to the local make-out spot, and run-ins with the local gang. This was the backdrop of high school circa the early 1960s and a period into which youth workers would eventually become an incarnational presence in high schools.

Setting the Stage for Modern Youth Ministry

With denominational youth groups struggling to hold on to their teenagers and the evangelistic youth rallies no longer holding the same magnetism they once had, something had to change. And change it did. Northern Baptist Seminary teacher Torrey Johnson was present at what turned out to be a rather large meeting that convened in the summer of 1945 to discuss the formation of an organization. At that meeting were a number of people who'd been practicing rally-type evangelism and those who'd emerge as key leaders in evangelicalism, including a young Billy Graham, who'd become the first full-time field staff member of the newly formed organization, while Johnson was named president.

Thus, Youth for Christ International, as it was called, was formed to provide a structure for the missionary and evangelistic ministries that were sweeping the country.[3] The radios and rallies approach to youth ministry would peak in the late 1940s and eventually be discontinued by the 1960s, largely because the *American Graffiti* youth culture had long since moved on.

There have always been different approaches to youth ministry, many of which don't make national—or even regional—headlines. Even so, each of these will still make an impact—however small it may seem—on both youth and adults. Such was the case around the period of the radios and rallies. Dotting the landscape from Illinois to California, and from Washington to Canada, were informal Bible clubs, formed for the purpose of being an "incarnational" presence for Christ in the high school. Fellowship of Christian Athletes, High School Born-Againers, Dunamis Clubs, Student Venture, Inter-School Christian Fellowship (a high school arm of InterVarsity), as well as a number of other ministries slowly rose up with variations on a theme—a club approach. One club, however, was quite influential in developing leaders for a movement—the Miracle Book Club.

Founder Evelyn McClusky was asked to teach the Bible to a group of high school students in 1933. The request seemed reasonable enough, and soon that one group spawned five. The Miracle Book Club was born. McClusky was then asked to write an article about the experience. It was so well received that within a year, a hundred more clubs were formed. A book soon followed the article, which explained the style and structure of the clubs. And as you'd imagine, the number of clubs swelled to more than a thousand, and all were located near high schools—but in safe or neutral places.

Salvation, victorious living, and becoming Christian "conversationalists" were among the primary goals of a Club, and it's the fine-tuning of these early impulses that would emerge years later as important building blocks for principles of youth ministry—both in the church and in parachurch organizations.

This growing "parachurch" club attracted stellar people in key local leadership positions, many of whom went on to establish the club methodology for what was to come (including some of the clubs mentioned above). One such person was Jim Rayburn.

Clubs and Camps[4]

Going to high school was now commonplace—so much so that if asked, teenagers probably couldn't remember a time when it wasn't. With the creation of the new label of "teenager," and as young people were increasingly being targeted as consumers, a new youth culture was emerging.

According to Dean Borgman, "One adult encountered and anticipated this culture more vibrantly than most."[5] Sensing a call to ministry as a young student, Jim Rayburn's learning curve included going where the youth were, outside the church walls, to listen and learn. From this unconventional approach, relationships were formed and the ideas for a new methodology emerged. Rayburn is well known for believing that it's a sin to bore teenagers; and as much as any evangelist before him, he wanted teenagers to hear the gospel. His conversational approach to speaking was distinctive and different from the rally speakers of the day. It was a quiet approach that understood the changes in adolescent culture, and its pace resembled a storyteller's timing. With what he was learning, Rayburn formed Young Life in 1942. He'd go on to forge a high school methodology that would be honed and refined into the Young Life movement.[6]

Rayburn's approach to youth ministry was essentially an effort led by adults to lead uncommitted students into a relationship with Christ. This stood in contrast to other clubs of the time but came out of Rayburn's time and experience with the Miracle Book Clubs. Young Life clubs were focused on evangelism. Its congregation would be the high school, and its declaration would be an emphasis on "winning the right to be heard." It was what we've since come to know as a process of "incarnational ministry"—a staff person or volunteer makes contact with a student, builds an integral relationship, and in the context of that relationship, life (and the gospel) is shared.

Then came the trip to Star Ranch—Young Life's first camp. In a day when the simple tent and sparse surroundings defined most Christian camp and conference grounds, Rayburn believed in upping the ante with the goal of developing the "classiest camps in the country."[7] Camping formed an integral part of the Young Life mission right from the beginning, using the camp experience as a capstone to the club program. From Young Life, many leaders would learn and be schooled in a philosophy of camping that would impact camping ministries years later. All of this became the fertile ground on which youth ministry would be planted for decades to come.

Youth for Christ was still heavily involved with evangelistic rallies while Rayburn was developing the club and camp strategy. YFC did have clubs in those early days of the '40s and early '50s, but their method proved problematic (the clubs, which were for fellowship and growth, were too attached to and dependent on the rallies). By the mid–'50s a change was needed. As the '60s dawned, the rallies had been discontinued, and adolescence had come into its own. YFC responded with an innovative club strategy and format that they were tagging as "2 plus 2."[8] Two meetings a month focused on evangelism (Impact), and two meetings a month focused more on growth and discipleship (Insight). Together, they were called Campus Life. Adult leaders and staff were limited to a few high school campuses to allow them time and opportunity to meet and build relationships with students in the high school, especially student leaders.

Well-received, this new style of youth ministry was having an impact and would continue to form and shape youth ministry through the '70s and into the '80s. The relational skills a person needed to connect with a new type of teenager were becoming evident because the teenager had changed. Adolescence was hitting its full stride, and the perceptive youth worker was taking note.

"I'll pick you up at 7," he said. And next Wednesday morning there was a knock at my door and off we went. There we sat with huge mugs of coffee, sometimes eating breakfast but mostly dunking donuts in what could be called a greasy spoon joint by some but was (and still is, of sorts) an institution in our city. We each brought the "workbook" we were supposed to go through, but over our first breakfast we quickly discovered that the workbook thing wasn't going to happen. So the "youth worker" did what came naturally and went with his instinct—we dropped the book, and the agenda came from life lived. The point was discipleship, but the jury was out in the minds of those the youth worker had to report to regarding whether this "coffee-and-donut thing" would yield the proper and intended outcome.

Par for the course in the mid-'70s, in which parachurch ministries led the creative charge to youth. But things would soon change.

Connections

When John Hughes sat down to write *The Breakfast Club* (1985), high school was looking rather different than it did in *American Graffiti*. The idea for the film must have been unconvincing to potential producers at first: five teenagers who don't know each other very well spend an entire day in detention together and basically do nothing but talk. But that's exactly how we notice that something is different.

Even though each of the five main characters still represents a type of teenager reminiscent of the '50s and '60s—Bender (Judd Nelson), an embattled working-class delinquent/punk/rebel; Claire (Molly Ringwald), the popular, pretty prom queen and rich girl; Andy (Emilio Estevez), the "sporto" wrestler-jock; Brian (Anthony Michael Hall), the brainy geek-nerd; and Allison (Ally Sheedy), the basket case, loner girl—the difference can be seen in how they are portrayed on film.

While the underlying teen angst simmers in *American Graffiti*, it comes close to a boil in *The Breakfast Club's* portrayal of youth in a sort of group therapy session about parents, popularity, sex, drugs, sports, clubs, wealth (or lack thereof), and suicide. While neither *The Breakfast Club* nor *American Graffiti* represents all varieties of the teenage experience, nor all teenagers themselves, what we do notice is how the contours of adolescence—and the culture that surrounds teenagers—has changed.

Some churches were now beginning to notice that things in the world of teenagers had changed, with many realizing the need for youth ministry beyond the Sunday school hour.[9] Youth groups started to increase in number, and churches began hiring youth pastors—many of whom had been on staff with parachurch ministries. As youth culture became increasingly fragmented, the relational skills to connect with teenagers and the style of ministry that many of these youth workers had honed in their parachurch days were seen as innovative and beneficial.

Youth ministry was maturing in style and substance as these newly hired youth pastors brought all that they'd learned from their parachurch roots into church youth ministry. The job, however, was more encompassing than what they were familiar with. They were now responsible for the care, education, and evangelistic concerns of youth within the church, on the fringes of the church, and out in the community. In spite of such a broad scope, it was the youth workers' ability to connect in relationship and to shape relationally focused ministries with teens that provided the greatest potential for impact.[10] This relational focus and drive slowly became a commodity of sorts, and it was supported by resources, seminars, and training organizations. And eventually it resulted in a program-focused ministry to youth.

Youth Ministry in a Branded Age

Current program-driven youth ministry has a tendency to be pragmatic and reliant on models. Youth ministry models now dot the ministry landscape. But when they're left unchecked, they can become sources of entertainment supported by a consumer state of mind. Whether the model is in the form of a funnel, pyramid, diamond, or concentric circles, youth ministry models aren't necessarily the problem. They're helpful and do provide a healthy compass for effective ministry.

The problem is twofold. One, the church has adopted approaches to ministry that further marginalize youth and uncritically buy in to marketplace versions of adolescence. And two, the tendency is to embrace a one-size-fits-all pattern of thinking with an eagerness to adopt and apply successful models without much forethought about one's own context—youth, families, congregation, local community and so on. A reliance on models can result in youth workers not doing the necessary "on the ground" theological thinking and contextualizing that's needed for ministry in their setting and with their youth.[11]

One of the interesting observations made by Mark Senter, in his study of the history of youth ministry, is what happens to innovative methods. In an attempt to keep youth—and sometimes out of a desire to attract them—churches would adopt and often adapt the new methods of the parachurch organizations. In this imitation of ideas and methods, the core or substance of the model would be changed or exchanged in some way to fit the context of the church, thereby weakening the uniqueness and the strength of the model—and at worst it's reduced to forms of entertainment.

This can be seen in what happened with both the Sunday school and Christian Endeavor. Once appropriated by the church, the Sunday school became concerned with only the Christian education of the church's youth and lost its impulse to reach out. Similarly, when denominational youth societies imitated Christian Endeavor, they weakened the strict membership pledge and accountability that characterized the movement, thereby weakening the very thing that made it work in the first place. The same thing happened when churches began adopting the highly relational and evangelistic club models of the parachurch ministries, using them to merely sustain their youth groups.[12] The evangelistic impulse was largely replaced with a protectionist impulse and a desire for discipleship focused chiefly on youth within the church—which often birthed programs shaped more by entertainment (a consumer value) in the hopes of keeping youth in the church.

Problems with the Church's Response to Adolescence

In the last century we've seen the concurrent rise of adolescence and formation of organized youth ministry. Adolescence has been effectively commoditized, and teenagers have become target markets and branded consumers. With the birth of "cool," the teenager, and all things adolescent came the need for the church to respond. And respond we did, with creative youth ministry approaches—along with their unintended outcomes. Mike King, in *Presence-Centered Youth Ministry*, identifies these unintended outcomes as dysfunctions. He recognizes the twin problems of succession (passing on the faith) and decisionism (the nature of conversion) as issues that all youth workers need to continually address regardless of whether we're in a church or parachurch context.

A related dysfunction, according to King, is an unbalanced view of tradition. His point is that there is a serious lack of connection to a deep historical tradition of meaning in most youth work that needs attention. King notes that, "Tradition, creeds and practices are much more easily respected as family heirlooms by current adolescent Christians."[13] There is a rediscovery of the Christian practices, creeds, rites, and rituals that have anchored the church for centuries among both adults and youth that's encouraging.

And lastly he identifies age segregation as a significant problem needing our attention. He rightly notes that it removes one of the most effective practices of spiritual formation—interaction between the generations. "Unfortunately, much of youth ministry practice places value on creating youth centers and programs, resulting—by default or intent—in separated generations."[14] And like the culture around us, youth workers forge paths for teenagers that take them away from adults, thereby contributing to the creation of "a tribe apart," rather than movement toward adults.

King believes each of these problems is rooted in an inconsistent understanding of classic Christian formation. He's right. And these dysfunctions of youth ministry are also rooted in an uncritical acceptance of adolescence as prescribed by culture, rather than an informed approach rooted in an understanding of historical Christian formation, which includes the larger narrative of purpose and vocation. And without that, teenagers come to believe there is no greater claim on their lives other than their own ambition and the belief that the one with the most toys wins—a belief that reverberates throughout their world (and one brought into sharp focus and without apology in commercial tag lines like this one from a local pool and spa company . . . "Gotta Have It").

Three Approaches

Don Richter has outlined three types of responses to adolescence that have been adopted by the church: protection, self-actualization, and tribal initiation.[15]

PROTECTION

The Sunday school movement identified youth as a stage of life that required its own graded and segregated curriculum. Society placed growing import on the new views in psychology, so this adult-led, sponsored, and segregated view for activities and programs was reinforced. Churches and congregations further accommodated their ministries to a youth group model (from Christian Endeavor to youth societies to youth fellowships organized at local, regional, and national levels). And current approaches to youth ministry immerse youth in adult-led and sponsored youth groups—typically entering during the middle school years and leaving after high school. This model, according to Richter, actually provides a holding environment for adolescents in which activities "rarely focus on the social practices and occupations of the adult world."[16]

Pete Ward, in *Growing Up Evangelical*, describes the notion of protection as a function of safety arising from the generalized fear that exists in the church toward the world beyond the church, including the current youth culture and the issues associated with it (peer pressure, music, fashion, and sex). So youth workers create places of safety for the youth of the church and away from these issues. The problem is the unintended outcome: the creation of a parallel universe—in the form of an alternative youth subculture—with its own fashion, music, pressures, heroes, festivals, and consumer products. And all this is driven and supported by the larger culture's consumer and market values. A separate subculture lessens the need to engage the real world and isolates teenagers even more, resulting in a dependency rather than healthy growth.[17] Furthermore, this dependency, when left unchecked, morphs into a kind of domestication "when the implicit curriculum admonishes youth to play it safe and stay out of trouble."[18] In other words, the concept of adolescence and the teenager are accepted uncritically and at face value, providing neither a good anchor in a tradition nor the space to explore new ideas and practices.

SELF-ACTUALIZATION

Standing squarely at the other end of the continuum is the response of self-actualization. Richter suggests that this is a more popular response among liberal Protestant churches. (Similarly, protectionism would likely be the more popular response of the conservative and evangelical churches.) This response would encourage a private spiritual quest, suggesting that youth need to be free to form their worldviews apart and distant from the church's tradition in order to reclaim tradition as adults. This rests on the developmental notion of teenagers needing to differentiate from adults and social roles. Then once their identities have formed and adulthood has been entered (especially once they're married and have kids of their own), they will return to the church.

TRIBAL INITIATION

If the first response is overprotection and the second is akin to a sanctioned period of abandonment, the third response identified by Richter stands in a more balanced location. It's what Richter calls tribal initiation. It's the responsibility of the faith community (that would be more than the youth pastor and youth group) to encourage the ongoing faith formation of its youth (meaning more than just the years in youth group). Tribal initiation is about recovering the concept of vocation for youth, the making of meaning, and the experience of the "whole" community of faith and adults as youth ministry.

Richter writes, "Youth can be who God calls them to be not by defining themselves in terms of youth culture or youth groups or youth activities, but by defining themselves as human beings who are summoned and drawn to particular commitments."[19] Forming teenagers according to this response involves an extended, challenging, high-expectations initiation process that will ultimately protect and release youth with a sense of purpose and a robust identity rooted in a Christian sense of vocation.

In *Practicing Passion: Youth and the Quest for a Passionate Church*, Kenda Creasy Dean convincingly argues how the church has essentially tried to manage the behavior of youth in an attempt to bring about spiritual formation and transformation. Dean focuses on the characteristic of passion in adolescence and how in the church we attempt to tame and domesticate it. Her belief is that by domesticating adolescent passion, we are removing a God-given life force that actually does the opposite of what the church wants. For if teenagers cannot find and use their passion in the church, they will find and use it elsewhere. Whether that passion is found in experimenting with at-risk activities or the more-accepted and encouraged outlet—buying stuff—youth are being consumed by things and the shallow veneer of life offered by our consumer-mediated culture.

"Much of what goes by the name *advertising*," says former advertiser-turned-church-planter Alan Hirsch, "is an explicit offer of a sense of identity, meaning, purpose, and *community*."[20] Hirsch has come to view consumerism as a major challenge to the gospel and a menace to the viability of robust faith. Because of the crowded marketplace, advertisers have become more and more competitive and have even co-opted theological ideas and symbols in order to sell (e.g., *Buy this and you will be changed!*). With little resistance countering these tactics, and youth ministries feeling pressure to compete with the marketplace offerings (and maybe even sometimes with the church down the street), it's no wonder that the passion Dean speaks of tends to be tamed, domesticated, and reduced to a list of good and bad behaviors.

The power to turn their world upside down—the power for spiritual formation, Dean says—comes when the church connects the passion of the adolescent with the passion of Christ.[21] We believe this impulse, this connection, is at the core of what Richter speaks of as being tribal initiation—and a youth ministry that captures the vocational imagination and impulses of youth.

A Detailed Look

In the last five years, the lives of hundreds of high school students in the United States and Canada have been transformed by participation in Ministry Quest. We'll go there next to examine a case study about how a youth ministry process funded by the Lilly Foundation has offered some resistance to consumer culture and has transformed churches, a seminary, and—to some degree—a denomination by specifically "thinking vocationally" and focusing on the development of call with youth.

Discussion and Study Questions

1. What are the trends, as you see them, shaping youth ministry right now? What implications do these trends have on your future in youth ministry? What perspectives, ideas, or movements influence and inform your development in youth ministry?

2. Having a sense of how adolescence is changing and how youth ministry has responded can raise central questions such as: Who is youth ministry for? Who counts as youth (and who doesn't) in North American culture? Is the function of youth ministry to shield youth from the surrounding culture by creating an alternative, safe Christian version of culture? Just what is the point of youth ministry, and what is the grand call?

3. Consumption shapes the way one comes to church, one's faith, and one's identity—in the end it bends one's thinking, tilting it toward believing that everything exists to satisfy me as a consumer. How has this way of living in the world affected youth ministry? Further, a consumer-driven culture can bend worship into becoming entertainment, the church into a shopping mall (where we choose this program over that one), and God into a commodity—a consumable product. Have you noticed this happening? If so, in what ways has this shown up in youth ministry? What are we doing in youth ministry that inadvertently shapes a consumerist mentality (i.e., consumer formation) rather than a discipleship formation? Has this shaped how we do youth ministry and define "good" youth ministry?

4. Which of the three general responses to adolescence (protection, self-actualization, and tribal initiation) illustrated in this chapter describes your experience? Which of the three are you most famil-

iar with? How would you shape a response to adolescence that offers some resistance to consumer culture and resolves into an adult identity? What does a response like that look like in your context? How would that inform—and how should it shape—youth ministry?

Try this . . .

With two or three young adults who've been part of your ministry for a while, work together at developing a short, candid, compelling case study around a challenge or problem that each of you believes is central to youth ministry in your context. Then discuss together ways through the challenge or problem. The intent here is to encourage dialogue around the larger ideas of youth ministry as a way of attending to the deeper questions of what we do (rather than "How do we get better attendance at Sunday school?").

8

LIVES TO OFFER: YOUTH, YOUTH WORK, AND VOCATION

The kind of work God usually calls you to is the kind of work (a) that you need most to do and (b) that the world most needs to have done. . . . The place God calls you to is the place where your deep gladness and the world's deep hunger meet.

—Frederick Buechner[1]

We can live any way we want. People take vows of poverty, chastity, and obedience—even of silence—by choice. The thing is to stalk your calling in a certain skilled and supple way, to locate the most tender and live spot and plug into that pulse. This is yielding, not fighting.

—Annie Dillard[2]

On the first retreat, we examined the anatomy of a call, and I started to put together pieces in my life," he said. "And I found that as a Christian there was a bigger call on my life than the one that was being offered to me by the world." This college student was discovering that his vision of what "could be" was not only being challenged, but also enlarged. So much so that, "after focusing in high school on academics-for-a-job, I entered a Christian liberal arts college where I am no longer 'just' acquiring knowledge that is marketable, but I am learning how to think, how to ask questions, and how to seek after the answers."

What has begun for this young man is what Annie Dillard, author of *Teaching a Stone to Talk*, would call "stalking" a vocation. "This Ministry Quest journey has made me realize the problems of consumerism and capitalism that support values such as greed and self-interest. I would never have gotten to this place in my life if it weren't for that first Ministry Quest retreat." He was locating his vocational "pulse," as Dillard would say, and leaning into it, yielding, not fighting against it.

Dillard says a vocation is something "to be stalked in a skilled and supple way." At times it seems like vocation is elusive, often hiding in the busyness and ambiguity of crowded lives. Should I do this or shall I do that? How should I apply my vocation in this new setting? Now imagine what it might be like for that high school senior you know who faces not only these questions, but also a myriad of others—all at once.

Thinking Vocationally

Over the last five years, hundreds of churches and high school and college students have grappled with deep questions about calling and vocation while engaged in a process called Ministry Quest. What is it about this innovative process that causes teenagers to face questions of call and vocation? What is the thinking behind the process, and how might this help youth workers and other youth leaders to "think vocationally" in their ministries? To locate some answers, we'll unpack the Ministry Quest experiences of one denomination and its seminary as a case study, if you will, and the lessons that can be learned through it.

In our current culture, vocation is elusive—should I do this or shall I do that? There can be many voices speaking simultaneously to those questions or none at all. Research done in the late '90s, by the Mennonite Church USA, indicated that for young people, being asked by their congregation to consider a vocation in ministry was a major factor in their pursuing the pastorate as a vocational choice.[4] Thus, Ministry Quest was born as one way that local churches, a bi-national seminary, and an entire denomination could provide that "ask" component for young people.

A Case Study: Ministry Quest

Ministry Quest is one of the Lilly-funded programs connected to the Mennonite Brethren (MB) Biblical Seminary with campuses in Fresno (California), Langley (British Columbia), and Winnipeg (Manitoba). The Lilly Foundation offered grants to seminaries across the United States and Canada for proposals that fit the criteria for a project titled, "Theological School Programs for High School Youth." It combines congregational discernment, an understanding of calling and vocation (which is deeper than the local church "blessing" an inward call), ministry or service opportunities for the participant, targeted rite-of-passage events, intentional spiritual formation, and mentoring by an established leader. Broadly speaking, the goal of the project is to nurture in young people ways of thinking, practices, and disciplines essential to the Christian life and to encourage youth to think theologically about contemporary issues. The purpose is to release back into their communities a cadre of theologically minded Christian youth who are preparing for leadership in the emerging culture in whatever form that may take.

SHAPING INFLUENCES OF MINISTRY QUEST

The MB Biblical Seminary's Ministry Quest program is designed to help churches discern, develop, and "call" high school students into leadership. Ministry Quest, as the name suggests, is not a program as much as it is a journey for high school students to explore opportunities in pastoral, congregational, and missional leadership. It features leadership retreats, church-based mentoring relationships, a short-term ministry assignment, and a church ministry observation.

The project designers developed three components to the "quest" that are anchored in the seminaries' historical Anabaptist tradition: First, the need for students to be discerned and nominated by their local church; second, the focus on vocation and calling; and third, the mentoring experience that takes place through relationships in the local congregation.

First, the discernment and nomination process is tied directly to the value of community. Before a young person can participate, he or she has to be discerned and nominated by his or her local church. This program is not self-selecting, so a young person who believes he or she is a leader or is called to ministry must come through the local church; teenagers cannot simply put their name forward. The principle here is to make sure the young people who participate in the project come with the full blessing and support of their congregations. Discussions with these young people have revealed that it's often this sense of discernment from the local community that provides enormous encouragement and a sense of purpose for the adolescent who is trying to answer the questions, "Who am I?" and, "Why am I here?"

The second component is the focus on vocation and calling. During various retreat experiences, young people hear the call stories of about twenty individuals, spend time looking at biblical call stories, and reflect theologically on issues and ideas of vocation and call. The "quest" is rooted in the assumption that all believers are called by God to bring his *Shalom* to the earth. At the same time, there is a recognized need for called and gifted individuals to lead churches and to understand what vocation is and what it looks like. The program seeks to encourage high school students to discover their call and understand their vocation, whether it's to serve in full-time ministry or to serve and lead in the marketplace.

The final shaping component is church-based mentoring. The church provides a nomination as well as a mentor for the young person. This mentor could be anyone of the same gender as the student who is growing in faith, loves teenagers, and is interested in passing on life lessons. The project developers provide twenty-six sessions' worth of materials for the mentor and participant to follow and encourages both of them to continue exploring issues of vocation, calling, as well as spiritual formation, as they spend time together. In talking with Ministry Quest participants, we learned that the mentoring relationship (not surprisingly) is one component of the project that's made a significant and lasting difference for both the mentor and the students.

UNPACKING THE VALUES OF MINISTRY QUEST

In the first couple of years, students completing Ministry Quest were initially given a compass to mark their "graduation" from the program. The compass signified the beginning of their journeys of "stalking" their vocations, as Dillard puts it; and it was to remind participants that they would still need direction in the days ahead. Similar to a compass, a set of program values was established to provide focus and direction as the experience was shaped for students. These values emerge as leaders explore call, experience life-on-life transformation, support the local church, intentionally create community, and receive unique learning opportunities.

EXPLORE CALL

By calling these high school students "leaders," the local church community makes a statement and is, in effect, declaring: "We believe you are a leader today, not a 'future' leader or a 'young' leader, but a real leader today." This both affirms and communicates that young people are and can be effective leaders even while living through the issues and transitions of adolescence.

By exploring call and vocation, the program takes seriously two things: first, that these young people are exploring a lot of different options for their lives; second, that figuring out vocation and hearing a call is a *process*. Participants are figuring out who they are and how they stand as individuals differently from and independent of their friends or parents. They are exploring the idea of call and vocation and how that is connected to an individual and rooted in a community.

One method that models this value is to have students think through and present their story, framed as a call, to the rest of the group. A second method, one that's a major focus of the Setting Your Sail retreat, is a personal inventory that includes skills, values, interests, and spiritual gifts. This helps further define call. Another way to think through calling is to help participants evaluate what they are experiencing on the retreats as a way of teaching reflective thinking. Currently this is demonstrated by group participation in the Ignatian Examen each evening of the retreat.

Holding retreats on a campus of higher education also helps with personal evaluation and serves as an encouragement for participants to wonder where and if a college or university education fits for them. Another method is to build into the program a short "check-in" time at the end of each session, during which participants respond to the material in some way. Finally, creating purpose statements for each session with learning goals helps presenters and participants stay on track with where the session is heading.

EXPERIENCE LIFE-ON-LIFE TRANSFORMATION

A high value is placed on mentoring and the role of the local church in the transformation of a teenager. If young people can connect with adults whom they get to know and trust—who provide both challenge and support—then ultimately both of them will be transformed by the experience.

Leadership development with youth happens best through relationship. During the retreats intentional time is given to hearing and sharing stories, both from the students and from the staff team. Students are placed in small groups in which the adult leaders share their stories as well as facilitate the group time. Relationships also provide the real-time learning lab for both formal and non-formal observation by students, who can observe mentors in action (whether pastors in ministry or other adults in the workplace).

Another way of framing the "life-on-life" imagery is through the notion of discipleship. Ministry Quest also functions as a holistic discipleship process for students. Rather than speaking of discipleship as a twelve-week course or some kind of further Bible study, the program seeks to build into the lives of students' two important values: one, the importance of having a mentor; two, the desire to keep growing in faith. These two values are what frame an understanding of discipleship.

SUPPORT THE LOCAL CHURCH

Ministry Quest has its start and finish in the local church. To emphasize this value, participants must be nominated by their local church. The church also provides a mentor for the participant, someone from within the congregation or pastoral staff. Then it reaffirms the participant halfway through the program year and provides ongoing support such as a short-term ministry assignment.

In order to support the local congregation, the program staff provides two five-day retreats, the mentoring curriculum, a website with a message board, help and advice, and support during the year. Because they've received so many requests for resources, Ministry Quest has created resources that support the church in its calling and discerning of *any* leaders, not just high school students.[5]

INTENTIONALLY CREATE COMMUNITY

On the MQ weekends, a high percentage of time is spent helping the students connect with one another. Community is created by eating meals together, sharing in small and larger groups, as well as doing a range of leadership activities from ropes courses to games. "These people get me" seems a common sentiment from participants on these weekends.

In addition to the natural connection, the staff works hard to come up with intentional community-building activities that include a wide variety of opportunities to get to know one another. These activities include instruction on how to shape and deliver their own personal story, as well as having each young person share this "call" story with the group. During these sessions the other participants offer affirmation, reflections, and feedback to these stories, culminating in a time of prayer for the person. These sessions are influential events in the lives of the participants. Many begin thinking through the implication that God has actually been at work in their lives all along and then share their stories for the very first time. In a culture where true, reflective listening is a lost art, these sessions also provide a safe space for young people to be truly heard by their peers. This part of the weekend alone is very powerful.

Students also begin to deal practically with the reality of a global community. Because Ministry Quest draws from across the United States and Canada, this is often the first blended activity in which they've been so connected to youth from another country. The retreats are intentionally planned so that one is located in the United States and one in Canada. This arrangement allows students from both countries to be the "guests" and the "hosts" on one of the retreats, which adds to the sense of community as students travel together across borders learning to appreciate and value the differences of the other.

RECEIVE UNIQUE LEARNING OPPORTUNITIES

The entire experience is designed to provide teenagers a wide variety of learning opportunities. Students are challenged to "raise the bar" and push themselves intellectually and spiritually by fully participating in the program. From the moment students apply, there is an expectation of excellence and higher learning from this journey.

There are many ways in which these unique learning opportunities are played out. From an academic standpoint, students can participate in seminary classes and in seminars with seminary faculty in which they can explore call and vocation from a wide variety of theological and biblical perspectives. They have meals in the homes of seminary faculty and administrators, giving them the chance to see professors as real people, as well as placing them around food and hospitality (which deepen the conversations about life, call, and vocation).

From a practical standpoint, they're given opportunities to learn about ancient spiritual practices by participating in *lectio divina*, *ignatian examen*, a time of silence and solitude amongst the giant Sequoia trees, prayer, and Bible study. After the retreat ends, they'll participate in six observation events—times when they'll shadow someone in ministry in order to observe a variety of pastoral practices or shadow a mentor to observe vocation through another lens.

From a personal standpoint, they're given a professional career assessment that combines personality, values, spiritual gifts, and skills into one tool that gives valuable feedback to a young person's individuation. They are challenged to learn new things about themselves by engaging in a high-ropes course that stretches body, mind, and spirit. And they learn about other cultures through intentional cross-cultural experiences. And finally the relationship with a mentor—which may have been more common in an informal or nonformal way for youth in generations past—is today a unique learning opportunity.

Unpacking the Ministry Quest Experience

RITES OF PASSAGE

The rites of passage offered to youth in our mass-mediated culture lack any kind of coherence. This means that coming of age in our culture— which is heavily mediated by technology, consumption, media, and generally little significant connection with adults—leads to contradictory messages of what it means to be adult, what it means to be grown up, and what it means to live life with purpose (and this is only a small list).

Originating with French anthropologist Arnold van Gennep and refined by others (most notably Victor Turner), *rites of passage* describes a process of emergence—as in, how people emerge as "new" once they cross the boundary from an in-between space into a newly defined space. Rites of passage unfold in three stages: separation from the community of origin, a period of testing called "liminality" (transition), and reincorporation with recognition and celebration of new status.[6]

The Ministry Quest initiative is framed by two rites of passage events that attempt to follow the three classic stages of separation, liminal challenge, and reincorporation. They're also infused with meaning regarding vocation bringing depth and a better understanding of, to bring to life Buechner's words, "the place God calls you to is the place where your deep gladness and the world's deep hunger meet."

CHARTING THE COURSE

After congregational discernment, the first stage of the program is an autumn retreat called "Charting Your Course." It's geared toward an understanding of call narratives, as well as helping teenagers understand the importance of a deep relationship with Jesus. During the retreat, students are challenged to understand leadership in new ways and are provided with a theological vocabulary to assist them in describing vocation, call, and their experience with God. In addition, reflective times are built into the schedule to allow students to become more attentive to the voice of God. The goal of this stage is to help students understand vocation and what it means to be "called."

The first retreat is followed by thirteen sessions with an adult mentor back in the participant's local congregation. The focus of these sessions is for the mentor to walk with the young person as he or she grows in a relationship with Jesus. Then the mentoring sessions are followed by a second discernment process with the pastor, mentor, and student to determine if the second stage of the Ministry Quest experience would be beneficial. If all three agree, the student attends the second retreat.

SETTING YOUR SAIL

The second rite-of-passage retreat, called "Setting Your Sail," is an event focusing more on the individual and who that person is as someone who's been uniquely called by God. This event physically and mentally pushes students through experiential exercises such as a high-ropes course; it explores an understanding of spiritual gifts, temperament, servant-leadership, and theological insights; and it builds on what was learned during the first retreat.

An additional thirteen mentoring sessions, with a continued focus on the young person's spiritual formation, follow the Setting Your Sail retreat. And the experience concludes with a short-term ministry or service opportunity based in the local church.

COMMISSIONING

At the end of the one-year program, the congregation is asked to hold a commissioning service for the young person. The purpose of this event is to simply acknowledge the steps the young person has taken during the year. It's an opportunity to bless and affirm what the congregation has discerned and to send the young person back to his or her high school campus or on to college with the support and blessing of the church.

Lessons for Youth Workers

Often programs like Ministry Quest are held in a kind of "best-case" environment (i.e., the circumstances, people, personnel, and students are there because they want to be). Great teachers, stimulating content, motivated students—all clustered on a campus . . . all leading to the creation of a pretty good experience and significant learning possibilities to be sure. But such outcomes aren't limited to those places only—and the learning doesn't have to end when the experiences end, either.

What can we learn from the Ministry Quest case study that would encourage the transformation that's currently underway in youth ministry? What's in that experience that would help youth workers make the turn to think vocationally in youth work? What places can youth workers lean into as part of leading teens through consumer culture?

ONE, IT'S NOT ABOUT THE YOUTH WORKER DOING MORE; IT'S ABOUT THE YOUTH BEING MORE CONNECTED.

Connected to more adults in a variety of non-formal and informal and, yes, even a few formal ways. Remember that the Ministry Quest process is more about the connection with the mentor and the sending church community than it is about any kind of event. This kind of connection doesn't require a big budget or a youth building—just relationships in the adult world. (Bear in mind that these relationships need to be adult-like relationships and not the kind that keep youth in a marginalized or childlike role—because it is that kind of mature connection that helps youth truly grow up.)

Twenty minutes is what it took to sustain meaningful relationships with adults outside their families, said a focus group of graduating university seniors when asked to describe a teacher who made an impact on them outside of the classroom. The professor was expecting to hear the *Mr. Holland's Opus-* or *Stand and Deliver*-like stories of teachers and adults going way above and beyond the call, investing hours and hours of time with teenagers. While the students had no difficulty recalling adults who had made huge impacts, what the professor was most struck with was just *how little* these adults needed to do to have an impact. The students shared story after story of teachers or coaches or other adults who pulled them aside after class or practice for what was typically a conversation of twenty minutes or less. A follow-up on a question, an affirmation, simply checking in, or a simple "way to go" was all it was usually. While these were relationships sustained over time (think of all those adults who could do this again and again and again within the parish or congregation), the life and impact often came in those short hallway chats. It didn't take all that much time, and yet the modest involvement of these adults made a huge difference.[7] This ought to inspire and provide hope for any adult that connecting with youth is not always a daunting and consuming endeavor but rather is often within reach.

TWO, IT'S NOT ABOUT THE YOUTH WORKER DOING MORE; IT'S ABOUT THE YOUTH WORKER KNOWING WHAT OUGHT TO BE DONE.

What this kind of process illustrates is that the capacity to engage youth at a more significant level is well within the reach of any youth worker, congregation, parish, or parachurch organization—and in many cases youth workers may already be using bits and pieces right now. Things you may already be doing such as some form of discernment, mentoring, and retreats can be easily recalibrated with a vocational twist and infused with a new kind of meaning and purpose around call and becoming an adult.

THREE, IT'S NOT ABOUT THE YOUTH WORKER DOING MORE; IT'S ABOUT YOUTH RECEIVING THE KIND OF FEEDBACK THAT THEY THRIVE ON.

The idea is that feedback from adults and the challenge of engaging the adult world in real ways are both important and necessary functions that develop adult capacities and provide avenues to guide teens through consumer culture. From shaping a graduation year process of discernment to guiding youth to discover their vocation through a wide variety of personal inventories and community feedback, the reward of adult connection and relationship in these contexts can easily provide life-shaping feedback. Whether it's the uncomfortable or unpleasant part or the positive, affirming aspects, the feedback must be anchored in the real adult world. Stepping in to "protect" youth from loss, setbacks, and even failure often has the opposite effect in terms of not preparing them for life ahead. Churches that practice discernment regularly affirm students' passions in art, medicine, photography, or ministry, or what have you, and can just as often provide important feedback for them in terms of pursuing "this" or "that" direction.

FOUR, IT'S NOT ABOUT THE YOUTH WORKER DOING MORE; IT'S ABOUT CHALLENGING YOUTH SO THAT THEY CAN GROW UP.

One thing is sure . . . adolescence is a time of energy, and often an energy waiting to be engaged. The perceptive youth worker knows that doing things for youth, or giving them the latest and best "Whatever," or overscheduling them with endless activities doesn't help them grow up. What a process like Ministry Quest suggests is that youth want (and need) challenge—in other words, tasks just beyond their current ability . . . that stretch them beyond their current competency . . . that nudge them just beyond their comfort . . . that in the end leave them feeling *more* adultlike after they've been mastered. Youth ministries and even parachurch organizations could find ways to provide and infuse rite-of-passage meaning and challenge to what they're already doing.

FIVE, IT'S NOT ABOUT THE YOUTH WORKER DOING MORE; IT'S ABOUT USING THE TIME YOU NOW HAVE.

Experiences like those designed for the Lilly Foundation are actually much shorter with respect to time spent with and exposure to youth than the time and exposure with teens available to youth workers. Yet these programs have significant impact on the youth who participate. There's no way to guarantee that all youth will make the journey to adulthood, understand calling, and live lives rooted in the biblical sense of vocation. But there are ways—by using the time, relationships, and space already available to you—to confront the lure of consumerism on youth. By highlighting and shaping discernment as a way of life, youth workers can provide a counter-cultural corrective to the unfiltered messages that a consumer-driven culture espouses.

Stories Worth Living

One young person phrased the impact of the process in this way:

> One of the key ideas awakened in me is a desire to understand and
> pursue God's calling for my life. While I didn't recognize it fully when
> I was in Ministry Quest, nor do I fully understand it now, that call was
> to give the whole of my life to God—and not out of my ability to give it,
> but out of recognition that it has belonged to God the whole time. One
> of the ideas that caught me was that youth are trained by culture how
> to consume rather than how to produce. It seems that a life centered
> around consuming is in marked contrast with a life of sacrifice to God.
> Yet we are led to a life of consuming by a flood of unfiltered informa-
> tion. I was challenged to expand the way I thought about my life and
> about God, to have an imagination that could begin to capture a bit of
> what God was capable of doing with my life. This process of learning
> to think better, which I'll continue using, is a part of having the right
> filters to wade through all the information available to us. Having the
> vision to see what the messages I get from the media, from friends, and
> from the attitudes of modernity and postmodernity are really saying is
> the beginning of understanding who I really am apart from the values
> society places on me.

What this young person seems to be saying is that the experience
of this kind of process is both informing and shaping a life story worth
living. And it is there we next turn to hear and learn from youth who've
become challenged by the idea of leaning into stories worth living.

Discussion and Study Questions

1. How would you describe your vocation? What has been most instrumental in the process of discovering your vocation and discerning your call?

2. How is ministry discernment practiced in your church community? If it isn't practiced, do you see a value in adopting such a practice? What about the question of vocation—how is it discerned with the teenagers in your community? It's said that *calling* is one of those "universal quest" themes that resonate with all of us (e.g., "What will I do with my life? Does it count for something? What's my part? Where do I fit?"). A consumer-driven culture constructs a narrative for youth that's connected to *stuff*—wealth, fame, and celebrity reducing dreams to smaller stories centered on making purchases. Where does that narrative leave teenagers? How can youth ministry engage this universal quest with coherence, meaning, and direction for life? How would you engage youth as partners in the Kingdom, encouraging the use of their skills and abilities and deepening a faith that goes with them into adulthood?

3. Who have been your mentors? We often experience different mentors for different needs. Describe some of the lessons learned and the degree of empowerment you experienced through those mentoring relationships. (The idea of *different mentors for different needs* in youth ministry could be translated as *inviting adults to be with youth in significant ways*. How would you go about doing that?)

4. Which of the lessons for youth workers conveys the most hope for you? Why? Which of the lessons expresses the greatest challenge for you? For youth ministry? Why? In what ways can that challenge be attended to?

Try this . . .

Make a list of five Christian adults you know who exemplify a life shaped by faith and marked by a vocational sensibility that connects their purpose in life with the purposes of God. How would they describe and talk about their vocations? Talk about that with them and ask them to spend some informal time just being with your youth over the next school year. Start by having them hang around at a planned event or three to get a basic sense of your teens. And then ask them to look for, notice, and talk with the youth whenever the community of faith gathers. What you are shaping is an informal mentoring environment that encourages simple but profound friendship encounters between youth and adults.

9

STORIES WORTH LIVING: YOUTH MINISTRY THAT THINKS VOCATIONALLY

Purpose is a stable and generalized intention to accomplish something that is at the same time meaningful to the self and consequential for the world beyond the self.

—William Damon[1]

When we bring "vocation" out of its secular meanings and into its theological fullness as life lived in response to God's call, we glimpse an alternative vision for youth ministry.

—Dori Grinenko Baker and Joyce Ann Mercer[2]

So, what do you do?" You know that question. Whether you're coaching your kid's soccer team or sitting on a plane, that question is inevitable. And that question for mid-adolescents can take on a couple of variant forms—"What do you want to be when you grow up?" or, "What are you planning to do after school?" These are questions about the future, questions often focused on getting a job—about future paid work. Paid work is necessary and good, but to reduce vocation to such a narrow view is limiting, constraining, and shortsighted. Vocation is about more than a job and is more than a career in the future.[3]

Vocation for youth is about a response to the work of God. It's about not only what they may want to do "when they grow up," but also who they are now, and what they have to offer now. And to use Damon's words, it's about something "meaningful to self and consequential to the world beyond."

Sophie and Bob

Sophie sensed God's call. An eleventh grader who was active in a couple of sports, as well as Campus Life and the youth group, Sophie had an engaging personality and self-confidence that caught the eye of her youth leaders and the church leadership. The church had a "Leadership Discernment Committee" whose task was to identify and tap the shoulder of any potential leaders regardless of age. This group had already spoken with Sophie and begun the process of discerning a call to leadership on her life. As a part of this process, the church provided her with a mentor—an older, retired missionary who had served for many years in Zaire (now the Democratic Republic of Congo). This woman, who was the same age as Sophie's grandmother, met with Sophie weekly to explore ways to love Jesus more deeply. She also shared her story of ministry and call with Sophie.

Sophie attended her denomination's national youth conference. After a session during which those who felt God's call were invited to respond, Sophie ran up to her youth leader with eyes aglow. "This session really confirmed what you and the church have been saying. More than ever, I want to serve in ministry."

When she returned home, Sophie spent a long time debriefing her experience with her mentor, who continued to affirm her gifts and abilities and encouraged spiritual formation as key for development. At around the same time, Sophie began to help with the middle school group on Wednesday nights. The opportunity to serve younger girls was something she really loved, and she appreciated receiving feedback on her leadership from the youth pastor. Another marker came in the form of a "girls' night" event hosted by the church, which also stood out as further confirmation of the direction Sophie was contemplating.

On the final Sunday of summer, right before Sophie began her senior year, the church held a special service to recognize and commission Sophie as a missionary to her local high school campus. They affirmed Sophie's call from the youth conference, the work of the leadership discernment committee, and the confirmation from Sophie's mentor. During the service Sophie was called forward, and her mentor and pastor prayed over her, sending her out to serve.

Now, when Bob returned from the same national youth conference that Sophie had attended, he met with his youth pastor, Brian, to process the event. "I think God is asking me to be a pastor," he said. Brian explained the process that the church had in place to serve those like Bob who may be sensing call or seeking vocation. "First, you need to meet with the Board of Elders for a discernment meeting and affirmation. Then there is a development process you can begin. The Elders will find someone to meet with you as a mentor, and you'll meet with this person every other week to study, pray, and share together. And since I just finished my mentoring with Jeff, who is now gone to college, I'd like to recommend that you meet with me. How does that sound?" Bob thought that would be great.

Following the encouraging time with the Elders, during which Bob was highly affirmed in his process, he began to meet with Brian regularly. During this time Brian invited Bob to participate in a variety of ministries that Brian was involved in. Bob began serving in the youth group each week and once a month at the rescue mission downtown.

On the occasion of Bob's high school graduation, Brian, along with Bob's parents, created a rite-of-passage experience to encourage Bob to continue pursuing a vocational path. They asked the people who'd been significant in Bob's life to write a one-page letter to affirm and encourage him in some way. Bob's mom then created a scrapbook filled with all of these letters to serve as a signpost on his journey.

In addition, Bob's dad and Brian worked with six other men to create a special experience for Bob. As he walked a loop around a local lake, each man was strategically placed at various points along the trail. Bob's dad began walking with Bob and shared one piece of advice as they went. Then Brian was waiting at the next point on the trail, and he took Bob from there to the next man, sharing more advice along the way. This continued all around the loop with all eight men sharing advice with Bob. And the experience was followed by a celebratory barbeque and feast.

Upon high school graduation, Bob decided to attend a denominational college with the goal of becoming a youth pastor. On the Sunday before he left for college, his church commissioned him, affirming this direction and offering to provide him with an internship the next summer when he returned home.

What These Stories Can Tell Us

Sophie and Bob were part of a vocational culture: A culture in which the discovery of purpose and the support of vocation, especially among the youth, were front and center. Because of this value, both churches instituted ways that assisted in this process of discerning one's call. However, each was unique and organic even though they shared the same purpose. The faith communities that Sophie and Bob belonged to seriously invested in assisting parents and their teenagers to unearth a vocation and calling, not just a major for college or a job to pay the bills.

What does a young person look like after participating in a contoured path like that of Sophie or Bob? He or she will have—

- Become someone with a clear sense of identity arising from a discernment and call process by the local congregation or group of adults
- Walked with a mentor for a significant time and deepened his or her spiritual formation
- Participated in rites of passage events on both a large and small scale
- Had ministry or service opportunities in the context of a safe and caring environment in which he or she would have learned how to both fail and lead well
- Been commissioned by the local congregation and other adults to serve and to lead in whatever context was appropriate

In the end we would be preparing youth to navigate their way through consumer culture from a stronger, more stable position. Youth would enter the early period of adulthood with a greater sense of self and a more solidified identity, a deeper spirituality anchored by practices that sustain faith, an experience with adults (mentoring) that extends beyond the high school years, the recognition of various markers that demonstrate adulthood, and a life prepared not by a program but by accompaniment.

ACCOMPANIMENT

Coming from the Latin words *com* and *panis* and related to the word *companion*, the word *accompany* means "to break bread with." It's about journey, for "one becomes a companion by traveling the same road and sharing one's bread with others."[4] What we're learning through the stories and practice of the Ministry Quest project is that the path to purpose isn't walked in the abstract, nor is it walked alone. Accompaniment involves adults being present and attentive to youth, first and foremost, as well as attentive to the contours of the road being traveled. It's not a sequential developmental process; it's more organic and experiential. Vocation, purpose, calling, and even leadership capacity are shaped by these types of experiences: an understanding of call, discernment, rites of passage, mentoring, service (ministry) opportunities, and commissioning.

CALL

Culture would suggest to young people that their choices are unlimited—you can do and be anything you want. In the face of such wide-open possibility, the choices youth face are astonishing, often nuanced in complexity and sometimes with little in the way of criteria to help them make good and right choices. Is there an orienting center? Who or what calls them? What has the power to call them "to be and to do"? This is the heart of the good news of the gospel. As Deborah van Deusen Hunsinger wrote in "Vocation: A Joyous Task," "To be without the gospel and its orienting center in Jesus Christ is a bit like being a ship on a vast sea with neither compass nor rudder."[5]

In the context of a local church, young people who have their gifts affirmed and are "called out" by the congregation to exercise those gifts are people who will grow fully in their individuation. Due to the richness of diversity, there are unique opportunities within a church or parachurch organization to demonstrate a wide variety of vocational callings to young people, assuming the adults within these agencies have determined their own call for themselves.

In one particular Ministry Quest experience, the student, parents, and congregation agreed that the student should pursue his passion in electrical engineering. And then the congregation blessed the direction in the life of that student. Call becomes a community experience and function rather than an individual task in which a person determines her vocation. And in doing so, it's not that a community of people determines another person's vocation but rather, a community of people comes alongside and walks with the one determining her own vocation. In other words, determining one's vocation is most certainly an individual quest, but it cannot be done well in isolation or outside of the community's shared experience. Having the church call and stand alongside the young person gives that individual the room to wrestle with what the call of God means in her life for whatever she decides to do.

> I discovered more about my spiritual gifts than I ever have before. The gifts inventory didn't surprise me in any way; but just the focus we put on them was really great. Usually when I take an inventory, people just hand me a list and say, "Okay, here are your gifts—I hope you know what to do with them." In this process the focus was on developing those gifts. —Allison

DISCERNMENT

Being discerned by a congregation offers strength and confidence to an individual who might not feel particularly gifted. Knowing that a congregation is standing fully behind a young person can provide that extra bit of confidence to step forward on the journey of leadership or discovery of a life path.

In a time when most people are left to themselves to figure out their vocations, this component is particularly significant to an adolescent. This calling out and discernment actually becomes a significant marker toward adulthood for those in the midst of the experience. In a world in which those types of markers are quickly vanishing, a discernment process encouraged and carried out by a congregation becomes a significant signpost, a rite-of-passage occasion, for a young person. This is especially significant for mid-adolescents in that it demonstrates that others are seeing something in their lives that they may not see in themselves. Others are seeing and speaking into their calling, purpose, direction, and vocation—they are noticed, they *do* matter.

RITES OF PASSAGE

The nature of rites of passage was explained briefly in the previous chapter. What we learned is that it's essential that the rites offer a rich blend of challenge and support. Whether these come through times of ritual and blessing or the planning of liminal experiences, it's important that these events be designed with deep levels of both challenge and support.

One former student wrote about his own rite-of-passage experience:

When Barry asked me if I wished to join him for coffee, I wasn't surprised. Barry was my youth sponsor, mentor, and a good friend—a trip to the local coffee shop was a weekly occurrence for us. The only difference in this particular outing was it had a certain celebratory mood as it occurred just after my graduation.

At first our conversation was just like it was any other week—we talked about life, politics, and business. Several minutes later, however, my youth pastor, Scott, appeared. He sat at our table, and then Barry promptly excused himself. Scott and I had a brief chat—he passed on some words of wisdom upon my graduation.

Scott and I weren't too far into our conversation, however, when one of my dad's closest friends, Brent, arrived. The game of musical chairs—coffee shop edition—thus continued. Finally, at the end of all of this, my dad came. After Brent left, Dad explained to me what was going on. As it turned out, the afternoon of conversation with several of my older friends was part of a celebration of my graduation from high school. My parents thought it would be a good idea for each of these men to spend a little bit of time just chatting, passing on words of wisdom, and celebrating this milestone of my life. It was a pretty touching experience. Afterward the whole group of us gathered at home and had dinner together.

The evening wasn't yet over, however. After dinner my parents presented me with a binder filled with notes written from all kinds of different people in my life about all kinds of different subjects. There was a letter from my pastor, one from my uncle Chris about being a father, and even one from one of my favorite teachers from high school entitled "Doing Your Best."

When I reflect back on this graduation experience that occurred only four short years ago, I am struck by several things. First, I note how much can change in four years. Between now and then, I've lost touch with a large amount of the contributors and have even lost one to death. Also, the feelings that accompanied being freshly graduated and not knowing what the world would look like on the other side of high school have been at least partially forgotten.

Despite all of these changes, this red binder remains my most cherished book. It is a reflection of the community that raised me and helped me get through my teenage years. It also symbolizes the community that was there to celebrate with me as I closed that chapter of my life. This book honored my "inner man." It also provided me with a concrete object that I could refer to or even look at to remind me of where I was at in my life.

To this day, every few months or so, I open this book and skim through a few entries. There I am greeted by old friends and am met with the same warmth, love, and affirmation that I was when I first read this book. Although my graduation would have been a momentous occasion even without this particular event, it was definitely this act—orchestrated by my parents—that ensured that I wouldn't forget its significance.

MENTORING

There are many outstanding resources for youth workers that both frame the mentoring experience and offer practical advice on the "how-tos" of mentoring. We would recommend, however, that youth workers digest *Big Questions, Worthy Dreams: Mentoring Young Adults in Their Search for Meaning, Purpose, and Faith* by Sharon Daloz Parks.[6] The twentysomething years of emerging adulthood are increasingly recognized as being critical but perplexing, and having a sense of that next place teens will be entering should prove helpful in your ministry with them even now. And in her book, Parks urges thoughtful adults to assume responsibility for providing strategic mentorship and offers a workable rationale for the importance of mentoring communities beyond youth ministry that also provides direction for us now.[7]

The following account provides a window on the power of adults in the lives of youths:

In February of my eleventh grade year (2003), I first became acquainted with George. He was the grandfather of my friend Val. George had some sort of charisma that seemed to draw people to him. No matter where he went, he always made an impact—something unusual for most 85-year-olds. Every Monday after school, I'd meet him in his study for a time of reflection and prayer, and each time he'd present me handwritten words of wisdom (all of which I've kept to the present day).

As the months passed, it became increasingly obvious to me that I'd found gold in this relationship. He had a way about him that always made me feel valued. He never belittled my various teenage attempts to express my identity in long hair or an obscure wardrobe. In fact, I think he rather appreciated my odd appearance, as it reminded him of the different, but equally ridiculous, fashion trends of his youth. In George's presence, I always felt validated. No matter what I brought up with him, George would engage in conversation with me as if it was the most important thing in the world—even things as diverse as hockey, Winston Churchill, and George Orwell's *1984*.

Unfortunately, my friendship with George was to be shorter than expected. Almost a year to the day when I started my weekly meetings with him, George had a heart attack that he would not recover from. In fact, a couple of weeks later, George was no longer able to make it downstairs to his study or find the strength to write. As George grew weaker, however, his impact on me did not.

For the last week or so of his life, I found myself at his house every day. Whenever I arrived, he somehow found the strength to emerge from his coma-like state and ask me to read some of his favorite Scripture passages. I remember feeling so odd in the apparent role reversal in our relationship. Instead of being ministered to, I'd suddenly been thrust into the role of being the one ministering to George. But it felt as if George was passing the proverbial torch of his ministry to me—this was the last and greatest gift George gave me. It forced me to care for another person even in the face of death—something I've never looked at in the same way since.

George died peacefully in the comfort of his own home, surrounded by family. I was blessed to serve as a pallbearer and deliver a reflection at his memorial service. To this day I carry with me memories of George—his friendship, his wisdom, and his identity as a man of integrity. Together these all inspire me on my path to becoming a better man.

—Travis

SERVICE OPPORTUNITIES

Service and ministry opportunities are about two things. First, the young person is given a chance to demonstrate his or her leadership abilities by taking responsibility for a specific ministry event, program, or project. The obvious ones come to mind, especially in the case of high school students: camp counselor, the director of a VBS or other children's program, or a team leader on a student mission trip. The key is that the young person is stretched by the task of seeing something fully through to the end.

The second is a time and place for the young person to serve another person or group without necessarily being in charge. This could be working in a downtown food distribution center, visiting the elderly, or reading to children in an after-school program.

Service opportunities move an individual's focus away from self and place it squarely on others. Ministry opportunities, particularly for those who've grown up in a church setting, create movement from "head" to "hands" (and the doing creates movement from cognitive to affective), which changes the language of their faith. It begins to morph from mere words into a call to live it out, and the more fluent in their faith language they become, the more they sense meaning and purpose in lives lived differently than the ones a consumer culture offers.

In many ways Michelle's story of serving in a short-term mission organization is typical:

"God has an incredible hold on this village."

Michelle's Thai teacher (whose name is Wow) is just one example of the many believers who are enduring persecution because of their faith. Sadly, most persecution comes directly from family members. Before Wow knew Christ, her life was dramatically different than it is today. She had a hot temper, used bad language, and was involved in gang activity. But God transformed her life to the extent that everyone around her was in awe of the changes they saw. But for Wow's mom, it didn't matter. Even if Jesus did turn Wow's life around, she wouldn't have her daughter set foot in a church.

For two weeks Wow stopped attending the Friendship Center, the church plant in Ang Sila. But she couldn't stay away. She had to worship; she had to be in God's presence and have fellowship with other believers. Even members of the community tried to convince Wow's mother to let her go to church if church was what made her different! But Wow's mother would not concede. And although Wow's mom abused her physically and verbally, Wow considered it a small price to pay.

On the evening that Wow returned to the Friendship Center, she was playing bass for the worship band. Michelle says that suddenly Wow was gone from the stage. Her mother had come in with a large stick and demanded that she leave. At that moment, Michelle and her teammate Jillian started interceding for Wow, praying that God would intervene and not allow any physical, emotional, or spiritual harm to come to her. They learned from missionary Karen Sanchez that when Wow left the church that night, she went to a friend's house and later returned home to her mom. Her mom was angry, but she didn't beat Wow.

Michelle's voice is heavy with conviction when she talks about Wow's dedication to the Lord. "One person who holds fast to the truth can shake a nation!" she says. This past year Michelle witnessed many of her Thai friends endure persecution for their faith in God, but the trials they encountered only stirred up a greater love and commitment to their savior. Michelle's time in Thailand has significantly impacted her life, changing her view of what normal is, and challenging her to intercede for the unreached and the persecuted. Her desire is to live out this "new normal" in a restricted access area of the world, shining light and truth over a nation of darkness.

—www.MBMSI.org

COMMISSIONING

There is formational power and affirmation in commissioning. Think of that young student who's been called to the front of a church and prayed for as he or she prepares to go on a mission trip. That experience is one of blessing and affirmation. In a very real way, the person being "sent" represents the church in the new location. There is power in the prayers of the congregation for the person pursuing a vocation that will take him or her away from home. Commissioning also makes available requisite authority for the one being commissioned. They are the called out ones.

Here is how one church (College Community MB Church) in Clovis, California, approached a commissioning service for their youth and mentors:

Litany of Celebration

DISCERNING GOD'S CALL

Leader: [*Student's name*], *we have watched you grow and we see within you a love for Jesus, a desire to serve God, and a potential for leadership. We walk with you in your Quest to explore and discern your giftedness, your leadership, and your calling.*

People: [*Student's name*], we, your church, join with God in calling you to ministry in God's kingdom. We support your decision to dedicate time and conversation to deepening your relationship with Jesus. We bless you to ask questions and discover language that helps you process what it means to be a leader. May you find joy and guidance as you listen to the voice of God in your life.

L: [*Mentor's name*], we are grateful for your willingness to enter into this Ministry Quest mentoring relationship with [*student's name*], studying Scripture together, opening yourselves to the transforming power of the Holy Spirit, and being accountable to one another.

P: [*Mentor's name*], we offer you our blessings and prayers in your role as mentor. May you find joy and guidance as you listen with [*student's name*] to the voice of God in his/her life.

Ministry Quest Participants & Mentors from Previous Years: We have already participated in Ministry Quest, and we are excited to see you begin this adventure. You can look forward to hearing God's voice, knowing each other better, and going deeper in your faith. We bless you to open yourselves to God's work in your lives.

Student & Mentor for This Year: We gladly enter this new relationship, walking together in friendship and learning. We look forward to hearing new aspects of God's call. We will do our part to take advantage of this opportunity.

ALL:

> We covenant together, God helping us,
> to love the Lord with all our hearts,
> to love each other as ourselves,
> and to listen together to God's call on our lives.

> We commit ourselves to each other,
> opening ourselves to God's transforming power
> and through us as we represent God to the world.

> May our joining together
> mutually bless and strengthen us
> as we follow Christ together.

Youth Ministry That Thinks Vocationally

Reflecting on the experience of pursuing vocation, Kevin comments:

> It has caused me to rethink consumer culture by encouraging me to think seriously about a career choice—even to the point of where personal financial sacrifice would be required. Full-time ministry staff positions aren't the best-paying jobs out there, and oftentimes they don't offer a lot of financial security. But the truth is, following my vocation and serving through it isn't about feeling safe and comfortable. So, by encouraging me to take seriously vocation and the call to serve God no matter what "job" I do, this experience offered me a perspective that's very different than the one offered by consumer culture. In addition,

this experience was really helpful in my own development as an adult, in that those within the program took me seriously. I felt supported, encouraged, mentored, and blessed to consider a range of vocational options, and I felt encouraged and affirmed when I chose to pursue ministry.

A few months ago, I took to lunch the man who'd been instrumental in my own story. Carman Ruggeri is not your typical pastoral success story. He never finished college, and he came to ministry from working in a grocery store. But he's had tremendous impact on numerous people in kingdom ministry today. I asked Carman a question that had been bugging me for a long time, "Why me?" I wanted to know why Carman and the senior pastor had kept after me and encouraged me into the path of ministry when I was a teenager. Carman said, "We talked about how we thought you were the kind of guy who'd want to give his life to something with meaning, something that will last." Living in, through, and out of a sense of vocation will do that.

Discussion and Study Questions

1. To what extent does a sense of call and vocation come through the larger faith community and in what ways could and should that community shape and inform those decisions?

2. Have you come across youth such as Sophie and Bob as described in this chapter? What are the steps—or what is the process your ministry has in place—to assist their vocational development and help them understand and discern vocation from a theological perspective?

3. Sophie and Bob were part of a vocational culture—a culture in which the discovery of purpose and support of vocation among the youth was front and center. In what ways could you go about fostering an intentional vocational culture in your ministry?

4. Carol Lytch, in her study of teenagers and church (*Choosing Church*, WJK Press, 2004), tells the quintessential rite-of-passage story—the spring break trip to Panama City, Florida. It marked the senior year and acted as a rite of passage—even for those who didn't go. For many it was the first vacation away from parents and adults; they readily exceeded the limits they didn't at home (with some experiencing tragic results); and identities, status, and relationships were redefined as they incorporated their new selves upon their return. Can you identify and describe any significant rites of passage the youth you know would participate in? If there are no significant rites of passage that mark the lives of youth, they will create them. What do you think these made-up rites of passage are? What do they look like, and what pressures might be associ-

ated with them? What are some practical steps you could take toward adding rite-of-passage experiences (if you don't already use them)? What rite-of-passage events does your ministry have in place that could be infused with deeper meaning?

Try this . . .

Research the idea of rites of passage as a means of spiritual formation, identity development, and as a form of resistance to advanced consumer culture for youth ministry. This is a powerful idea that we have yet to fully recognize as a means of shaping ongoing ministry. We could single out an event or two to boost the rite-of-passage quotient and take a deeper, more sustained look into the meaning, implications, and journey connected with rites of passage as a possible frame for youth work. What does it mean to involve young people in ongoing practices that separate them from childhood patterns of behavior and adolescent self-absorption prescribed by consumer culture so they develop patterns of adult responsibility and identities rooted in the passion and presence of God? What does it mean and what would it look like to involve youth in a "liminal communitas"? And in what ways could we intentionally integrate formal and informal acts of real incorporation—the final phase—in ways that take us far beyond Youth Sunday and provide substantial clarity as they become adults with adults who've gone before them?

EPILOGUE

Some of the greatest moments in youth ministry happen when you grab somebody by the collar and say, "Hey, kid, come over here. You, try elementary school teaching. You, try nursing. You, . . ." In college I meet so many who are just desperate for an adult to say, "You know what you are good at?" "You know what we could use from you?" They are hungry for that.

—William Willimon[1]

Finding a meaningful place in the scheme of things and having a sense of purpose in a large and interdependent world is manifest in a sense of vocation. Young people depend upon faithful communities of discernment and confirmation to provide developmentally appropriate experiences as they seek that place where their ambitions and aspirations meet the hungers and hopes of the new commons.

—Authors of *Common Fire: Lives of Commitment in a Complex World*[2]

A professor watched as a few hundred students listened to a representative from Teach for America. She walked onto the stage of this major university and said, "I didn't think anyone would be here tonight. But I can tell by looking at you that this is probably a waste of your time." This representative began her presentation by saying she could tell these were successful students who would have options upon options after graduation. She observed out loud that they could easily get a job on Wall Street making large amounts of money. "And I'm looking for a few people to go out and make less than $20,000 a year and work in some of the most violent, difficult school situations in this country."

She could tell just by looking at them that any of the people gathered in that auditorium could do better than that without breaking a sweat. "Two teachers in our program were killed last year. But I have brochures here, and if any of you wants to pick one up, help yourself." The professor watched as students pushed and shoved and jostled about to get their hands on a brochure.

One of the challenges facing youth workers, Professor William Willimon has observed, is that "it is counter-cultural work to teach young people to look for 'vocation' rather than a job."[3] But when given the opportunity to seek vocation, young people will rise to the call.

The Changing Shape of Adolescence

Thomas Hine concludes that we adults create the conditions in which young people face the task of building their lives—the process of coming of age. He suggests that we color their world and much of what they know with our own biases, fears, and joys. And he reminds us that in spite of doubts to the contrary, youth do tend to listen to and believe what their parents and other adults in authority tell them. "One of the most important, confusing, and even damaging things we tell them is that they are teenagers," writes Hine.[4] And he's right. What we tell teenagers about being teenagers shapes their experience of growing up. And what's most different about growing up today (compared to the turn of the twentieth century or even the 1940s) is that the major voices have changed—and so has the message.

"Once we understand that the teenager—this weird, alienated, frightening, yet enviable creature—is a figment of our collective imagination, the monstrous progeny of marketing and high school, all generations will benefit."[5] We know, however, that our advanced industrial consumer society has a vested interest in keeping youth young and adults forever young in a perpetual state of "planned immaturity."[6]

"Adolescence," writes Friedrich Schweitzer, "is no longer a well-defined period of transition with the task of preparing people for adulthood."[7] As we have seen, it has expanded in both directions—toward childhood (age compression) and toward adulthood, meaning it's now a ten-, fifteen-, or even twenty-year experience increasingly detached from any connection with the adult world. The resulting expansion and vagueness of the adolescent experience creates an increasing void during those years that will be filled.

Infection

Seeping into that void is a virus that's causing infection—a contagion, really, which fosters an attitude among people shaped by an ideological code. The code, or ideology, becomes fixed in the mind of society—even in our churches—and becomes the accepted "common sense" account of what it means to be a teenager, thus affecting both the way teenagers live and the way adults relate to them.

Remember, we simply don't question or critique this "common sense" understanding, so it naturally becomes what we reflexively think about youth. And then it becomes what we *believe* about youth, which, in turn, becomes what youth then believe about being a teenager. It's an ideology of youth out of which adults and youth generally live. In our advanced consumer-mediated culture, this ideology is stated as: Youth are primarily consumers, youth are supposed to be rebellious, youth are primarily self-absorbed, and youth are only peer-oriented.

Derek Melleby, of the Center for Parent/Youth Understanding, recently sat down with Dr. Tim Clydesdale, a sociology professor at The College of New Jersey, for a very short, yet compelling interview.[8] Melleby asked about the most surprising thing Clydesdale learned about teenagers from his research on the transitions from high school to the first year of college. Clydesdale responded,

> I would say it was how open teens were to talking to a sympathetic adult listener. It was as if they yearned for a sounding board—a listening and engaged ear—and once they found it in the interview room, they poured out their hearts. Neither their parents nor their peers provided an unfettered place in which the teens could talk; it seems that the adults in teens' lives were more interested in telling them something than they were in listening to them, and that friends were likewise so caught up in their own concerns they didn't listen very much either. This reveals something about American culture—that we nurture individuals so consumed with themselves that we as a culture are losing our desire if not our ability to listen. Even well-meaning folks like teachers, parents, and youth pastors get so caught up in conveying a set of ideas that they rarely let up on the barrage of information. Teens are drowning in competing claims for allegiance, and no one, it seems, is providing the time and space to sort through all of this.[9]

Can you spot the infection—where the virus might be at work?
From his research Clydesdale also observed that far too few teens'

lives are shaped by purpose, few demonstrate direction, and few recognize their interdependence with communities small and large. They don't think about what it means to live in the biggest house in the global village.

"Did you notice any difference with Christian students you interviewed, or would you say that this is true for most teens, regardless of religious affiliation?" Melleby asked.

"I found this to be true of most Christian students," responded Clydesdale, "even those who say their faith is 'very important' to them. It seems most Christian students want to keep their faith in a nice safe box: they attend church, they read the Bible, and they pray; but they largely pursue the same work-spend-borrow-consume lifestyle that their non-Christian peers do. Unfortunately, few of these youth possess the mentorship that nurtures this sort of faith development, and without it, the tug of work-spend-borrow-consume may ultimately prevail."[10]

Paying attention to the conditions in which we now find ourselves, assessing how we came to be here, and reflecting upon possible correctives was the direction of *Consuming Youth*. By moving in the direction of a new ideology of youth, we can encourage a more robust and discerning ministry with teenagers.

Antidote

An antidote is a substance or material that counteracts the action of another substance; it's something used to relieve or neutralize what's happening. What we're suggesting is that a new ideology of youth, and the experiences that support it, act very much like an antidote—counteracting the prevailing ideology of youth. We must begin to make shifts in the way we approach youth, and our thinking about what it means to be adolescent, and support those shifts with experiences that work to counteract the prevailing attitudes and cultivate and sustain a new ideology of youth.

WE MUST CHANGE OUR PERCEPTION OF YOUTH AS CONSUMERS TO A LIVED BELIEF OF YOUTH AS CALLED.—

And if we live out that belief, we will cultivate a culture that helps youth discern that call. A significant experience that both cultivates and sustains a deep change in this perspective is that of *discernment*. Imagine the power of a small gathering in which youth workers, teachers, friends, parents, and other adults who are closely involved in the life of a young person inform that young person about what they see. Imagine the power of that gathered group of adults speaking life into a young person as the living voice of the church. This not only would breathe life into that teen-ager, but would also be transformative for adults as their perspectives about teenagers are challenged and changed through such experiences with youth. As the young person begins to muck about with the meaning of what others have seen, discernment occurs and an understanding of vocation and call are made tangible. All of us need to begin telling young people what we see in them. And in so doing, live counter-culturally as Willimon says, teaching "young people to look for 'vocation' rather than a job."[11]

RETHINK MINISTRY ACTIVITY BY INVOLVING YOUTH IN THE PLANNING OF ALL ACTIVITIES AND MOVING YOUTH PROGRAMS FROM A MARKETING ORIENTATION TO ONE OF TRANSFORMATION.—

This change requires a deliberate and conscious shift from youth pro-gramming to youth transformation.[12] An ideological shift in our own thinking occurs, moving from "Youth as Consumers" (if we build it, they will come—and then we can grow) to "Youth as Asked" (if we inform them of options, they will provide feedback—and then we can serve them better) to "Youth as Empowered" (if we partner *with* them in every seg-ment of ministry, they will recognize need and response options—and then we can consciously put more and more decisions in their hands and facilitate their leadership).

Lean in to this conversation that author Joyce Ann Mercer had with a 16-year-old high school student. The Friday night drop-in youth club (sponsored by the parents as an alternative social gathering place for teenagers) was obviously important to Jana. "I wouldn't know what else to do on a Friday or a Sunday night," she said. She continues by talking about how it's just where she needs to be on a Friday night and how it keeps all the parents from worrying because they know where their kids are and what they're doing. "After all," she says, "kids do get into so much trouble these days." She goes on to talk about how really nice her youth pastor is. It was obvious that this relationship was important to her. Her take on his role is "to make sure we like to come, so that when we graduate we'll all still want to come back to church." At the same time, though, while she expressed enjoyment with the relationships, camaraderie, and fellowship she experienced with her peers in the youth group, she was "practically starving" for in-depth conversations of theological questions. "But in my youth group, we mostly go bowling," she said.

While reflecting on her conversation with this young woman, Mercer wondered, *What vocation does this church hold out for Jana to embrace?* There are many benefits and good things happening in the group, concluded Mercer, and there is nothing wrong at all with recreation and fun—both are essential elements for all kinds of ministry and ought to be present to some degree. Mercer continues, "It is apparent that much of what goes on there takes a defensive posture: youth ministry as a prevention for the troubles teens will otherwise get into." From the many conversations she's had with teenagers like Jana, Mercer observes that instead of inviting youth into important practices of faith—informed by such things as service, reflection, prayer, and so on—"the main 'call' to which the church invites these young people to respond to is the call to be entertained and to stay out of trouble."[13] When given the opportunity, many teenagers will engage with the big questions, dream worthy dreams, and be challenged by a larger call.

WE MUST CHANGE OUR PERCEPTION OF YOUTH AS ONLY SELF-ABSORBED TO A LIVED BELIEF OF YOUTH AS OTHERS-CENTERED.—

And if we live out that belief, we will cultivate a culture where youth and adults are involved in meaningful work together. A significant experience that both cultivates and sustains a deep change in this perspective is that of *service*. We are to be a blessing to others and to God. Yet there is a tension pushing and pulling between the self-serving ego and the others-oriented self. And to make matters worse, our consumer-driven culture markets directly to the desires of the self-serving ego. However, there are moments with youth we've seen where they are quick to realize that serving others is at the heart of the gospel. We've seen it, and we are sure you have, too.

To support and encourage those moments, Murray Baker, a former public high school principal who now leads a national campus youth ministry, suggests some practical ways that youth can live "Christianly" from the Sermon on the Mount, which describes Christians as "salt-seasoning that brings out the God-flavors of this earth . . . [and] light, bringing out the God-colors in the world" (Matthew 5:13–14, *The Message*). So, Baker suggests,

> In schools that deal with violence every day, Jesus says, "Don't hit back" and "Love your enemy"; in schools where so many get ignored, Jesus says, "Live graciously and generously toward others . . ."; in schools where anger is the norm, Jesus says, "Forgive"; in schools where "put-downs" are a way of life, Jesus says, "Don't pick on people, jump on their failures, criticize their faults"; when most teens think only of themselves, Jesus says, "Ask yourself what you want people to do for you, then grab the initiative and do it for them." And Jesus concludes with, "These words I speak to you are not incidental additions for your life. . . . They are foundational words, words to build a life on" (Matthew 7:24).[14]

RETHINK MINISTRY ACTIVITY BY REIMAGINING HOW WE THINK ABOUT SERVICE, AN IMPORTANT EXPERIENCE THAT BOTH CULTIVATES AND SUSTAINS OTHERS-CENTERED DIRECTION.—

Many youth groups already invest time from their school breaks and summers on mission or service projects either locally, nationally, or overseas. Instead of just a youth group project, reimagine it as something to include all ages. Specifically and with intention, the whole endeavor ought to involve adults who serve, work, worship, and play alongside the youth. These shared experiences build community faster than just about anything, with multigenerational relationships being forged that extend well beyond the life of the service project.

On the beach in the heat of summer camp, a young man says, "I just don't know what to do after school." Now, it's not that this seventeen-year-old guy didn't have options. Actually, swirling about in this young guy's mind were too many options, too much noise. As we sat and talked, he listed off this reason for that option and that reason for this direction. When asked what other adults had offered by way of their conversations with him about his dilemma, his response was, with a blend of humor and lighthearted sarcasm, "What adults?" Now, again, it's not that he didn't have adults in his life. His parents certainly were in conversation with him. But what he was saying was that there was something missing, a missing piece to the whole thing that he couldn't quite put his finger on. And yet, in the midst of the confusion and lack of discernment, this teenager chooses to spend his summer serving and working with kids at a camp for much less money than what he could have made elsewhere. When given the opportunity, many teenagers will lean into vocation trying to find a path to purpose.

WE MUST CHANGE OUR PERCEPTION OF YOUTH AS ONLY REBELLIOUS TO A LIVED BELIEF OF YOUTH AS RESOURCED.—

All youth want to feel competent and to contribute something. And Christian youth want to know that God is actually at work in them and through them. A life-giving and significant experience that both cultivates and sustains a deep change in this perspective is that of an *empowered sense of commissioning*.

"The most impressive entrepreneurial birthing center for the young that I have discovered anywhere," wrote Tom Sine in *The New Conspirators*, "[is] Launch, [which] was created by Carl Nash for Youth Unlimited (Toronto Youth for Christ)."[15] The group at Launch invites fifteen- to twenty-five-year-olds "to bring an entrepreneurial idea for a new kingdom ministry that God is stirring up within them. A mentor is assigned to work with each student to help them fashion their beginning dream into a bold initiative and helping them get it launched just like a new business start-up."[16]

Sine then tells the story of Ted Webb, a self-described nineteen-year-old "bike-aholic" who brought a dream to Launch that had taken root during a summer trip to Malawi. There he'd met pastors who had to walk two to three hours to visit church members because they didn't have ready access to any form of transportation. Africycle was born. Bicycles are donated, which are then repaired and restored before being shipped to pastors in Malawi. The containers used to ship the bikes are designed to function as small bike-repair shops. Spare parts are shipped along with the bikes, and locals are trained how to maintain the bikes. The income from these shops provides financial support for disabled and orphan children.

"I am convinced God could do much," concluded Sine, "through the creativity of our teens and twentysomethings if we help them give birth . . . to what God is stirring up in their imaginations, if we invite their ideas and innovation."[17] An *empowered sense of commissioning* that formal act of saying yes to youth, of granting authority, of blessing, of affirmation, and of prayer cultivates and sustains a lived belief of youth as resourced. When given the opportunity, many teenagers will lean into vocation choosing to live in that place where their ambitions and aspirations meet the hungers and hopes of others.

RETHINK MINISTRY ACTIVITY BY CHOOSING AND BUILDING SPECIFIC MOMENTS THAT OUGHT TO BE SIGNIFICANTLY MARKED AS A TIME OF COMMISSIONING.—

Many of these moments already exist (mission trips, going off to college, having significant responsibilities at school or work, serving on ministry teams, and so on). Oftentimes, though, a prayer is added at the end of a service, or a notice is placed in the Sunday bulletin, or a separate function is held just among the youth. Something, to be sure, but these small attempts rob commissioning of its power as part of a significant rite of passage.

WE MUST CHANGE OUR PERCEPTION OF YOUTH AS ONLY PEER-ORIENTED AND AGE-SEGREGATED TO A LIVED BELIEF OF YOUTH IN COMMUNITY.—

And if we live out that belief, we will cultivate and sustain a culture in which *rites of passage and an informal mentoring is the norm,* providing robust alternatives to the pattern we currently find ourselves in. Joseph Kett identifies that pattern as "institutionally segregating young people from casual contacts with a broad range of adults."[18] This pattern, which began long ago, leaves the authors of *Dancing in the Dark* to ask an obvious but necessary question, "How are youth going to mature except by contact with adults?"[19]

RETHINK MINISTRY ACTIVITY BY RESPONDING TO THE DEEP DESIRE OF YOUTH TO BE ATTENDED TO; WE ADULTS NEED TO LISTEN TO AND ENGAGE WITH THEM AS THEY ENDEAVOR TO BUILD MEANINGFUL LIVES FOR THEMSELVES.—

It's about encouraging simple and profound friendship encounters and casual contacts with adults (informal mentoring environments) at every level of the faith community—but specifically intergenerationally. It's more of an intentional shift in attitude and thinking than any kind of programmatic mandate.

Eugene Peterson, in *Leap Over a Wall: Earthy Spirituality for Everyday Christians*, reminds us that we've each had contact with likely hundreds of people who never looked beyond the surface of our appearance, or who first determined what use we could be to them before befriending us. Being in a group where we are treated as less than we are, Peterson says we then become less. And this happens again and again to many teenagers, which makes their need to receive attention such a profound desire. Then Peterson relates what the Jewish philospher Martin Buber once noted: "The greatest thing any person can do for another is to confirm the deepest thing in him, in her—to take the time and have the discernment to see what's most deeply there, most fully that person, and then confirm it by recognizing and encouraging it."[20] It's no wonder, then, that in his study about how and why so many of today's young people are failing to find a purpose in life, William Damon discovered that the first important step in achieving a path of purpose was "inspiring communication with persons outside the immediate family."[21]

In his discerning and soulful book titled *Contemplative Youth Ministry*, Mark Yaconelli tells a powerful story about Father James, his wife, Eli, and their small aging Episcopal church in a central Colorado ski town. We've paraphrased it here.[22]

> The youth ministry team from a 200-member congregation consisted of eight elderly adults who sensed a call and were guided by "home" as a theme and image for youth ministry.
>
> A young man died of alcohol poisoning after a night of partying and drinking with his buddies. A few days later James was in a coffee shop, wearing his white collar, when two guys in their early 20s came up to him and asked if he was a priest and if he did memorial services. He told them he did and invited them to sit down. Then he listened as they told him it was their friend who had died. They began talking about their lives in Colorado. They told James that they and many of their friends came from broken homes, and many of them went from ski town to ski town looking for work and parties. They talked about sleeping in cars and working odd jobs in this upscale resort town. James listened. They told him their friend was from New York, and that his parents had flown his body back home for the funeral, but none of them had the money to travel out East for the service. They asked James if he could hold some sort of memorial service in town so they could mourn the death of their friend. James agreed.
>
> James then met with the youth ministry team, and they readily agreed to help prepare and serve food for the young people attending the memorial. On the day of the service, the team showed up early and transformed the fellowship room into something resembling a visit to

your favorite grandmother's house. They had three kinds of soup simmering, sandwiches cut into triangles, and fresh-baked cookies placed on platters around the room.

More than 100 young adults, ages 16 to 25, gathered in the sanctuary wearing baggy pants, knit hats, worn military fatigues, and other rough snow gear. James ran back to the fellowship hall and told the youth ministry team that more food was needed. The group hurried to the grocery store and soon formed a sandwich assembly line, while 68-year-old Glenda made more soup. At the close of the service, James invited the youth to stay for food. Every one of them stayed. And for the next five hours, the young "ski bums" ate soup and sandwiches and poured their hearts out to the listening adults. One woman later told Yaconelli, "Most of us have lived long enough to have friends and even close family die, so we knew how to listen and be with these kids who were in grief."[23]

The adults noticed that many of the young people had holes in their shoes and clothes. They went over to the long-neglected "donation" box in the narthex of the church and found clean pants, tennis shoes, and warm jackets. They brought them to the fellowship hall and offered them to the youth. When the evening finally started to wind down, one of the young men asked if they could come to the church again sometime.

That night, after clean-up, the youth ministry team gathered. They talked about the great need for food, friendship, and clothing among these particular youth in their town. They talked about how much they'd enjoyed talking and being with these youth who often appeared rough and distant. They prayed. They listened to how God was calling them to serve. An idea emerged. Each month they would have a night just like this—a night when they would serve good food, hand out clothing, and spend time just hanging out with and listening to these youth in their community.

A small aging church simply responded to the deep desire of youth to be attended to. Guided by "home" as a metaphor for engagement with youth a variety of adults—many much older—served, shared a meal, and listened to youth as they tried to make sense of life. In this case it wasn't fancy (and doesn't need to be) and was pretty casual. It was about simple-yet-profound friendship encounters that connected youth with adults.

Reimagine

Change is in the air, and many youth workers are developing meaningful and creative experiences for their youth. We all applaud these efforts loudly and enthusiastically. But still, there is always room to maneuver, grow, and change at the edges. There might be some pockets that concentrate almost exclusively in entertainment and consumer activities: bowling, pizza, and trips to the mall, and perhaps even that segregated youth worship time that's beginning to resemble more concert than worship. Yet a steady youth ministry diet of this sort reinforces our culture's reductionist definition of adolescence and its consumer orientation, and it's of little help when preparing youth for adult life or shaping a faith that lives beyond the youth group experience.

"Our role," Mike Yaconelli once said, "is not to create nice, compliant American citizens ready to get a good job and have 2.4 kids."[24] Instead, we are to introduce young people to Jesus and the kingdom of God. We are to walk alongside them as they unpack that story and find their place in it. We are to live a different belief about teenagers, building a canopy, if you will, under which youth can discover vocation and meaningful lives, be deeply engaged with adults, and be captivated by a new and different story for what "becoming adult" means.

The good news is this: Any youth ministry, any congregation or parish, and even parachurch organizations of any size have what's needed to cultivate a new ideology of youth. We know that teens are more than the script our consumer culture lays out for them to live by. We know that God has purposed teenagers to be more than consumers and more than the images that brands hold out for them to desire. We know that teens are more than the colleges they may or may not get to attend. And we know that vocation as a lived response to what Jesus has done captures and holds teens' imaginations and ignites their souls more than owning the next new gadget or being entertained ever will.

The hopeful message is this: All youth ministries, all congregations and parishes, and parachurch organizations of all sizes have what's needed to shape the sustaining experiences that support a new way of thinking about teenagers and that serve to lead teens through consumer culture. The challenge lies not in reinventing an old youth ministry model or even creating a new one but in simply rethinking, reimagining, and paying attention to what we're already doing. In the end it's about living with and walking alongside youth, making them an integral part of the community, not segregated from it. It's about being the deep and rich and whole community Jesus has called us to be.

And that is well within reach.

Discussion and Study Questions

1. "Most teenagers," observes Kenda Creasy Dean in her book *Almost Christian* (Oxford University Press, 2010, 151) "have few structured opportunities to eavesdrop on the grammar, vocabularies, habits, virtues or practices of mature Christian adults." How can youth ministry arrange for such eavesdropping opportunities for youth? What would that look like?

2. While the ideas of this book are not intended to suggest we can somehow end consumer capitalism, we did set out to suggest that the rise of a market economy (consumer culture), the invention of adolescence, and the rise of youth ministry occurred at roughly the same time and that our response to adolescence (youth ministry) has been shaped more by market, consumer, and cultural sensibilities and beliefs rather than by what teens might really need to move into adulthood. In what ways have our approaches to youth ministry been shaped more by consumer and cultural understandings of teenagers? What is it that teens need to move into adulthood well? In what ways can youth ministry provide an environment that supports that transition?

3. In *Consuming Religion* (Continuum, 2005) Vincent Millar suggests that if theology is to respond to the challenges posed by a consumer culture, it must attend to the structures and practices that connect belief to daily life and help communities find ways to sustain faith practices in the face of the creeping erosion of globalizing capitalism. We have suggested a few things in this chapter and now turn to you . . . what must youth ministry become in order to respond to the challenges posed by consumer culture? What must youth ministry attend to in order to counteract the prevailing attitudes and beliefs about teenagers and sustain a new ideology of youth?

Try this . . .

In the introduction we wrote that this book would be more suggestive than prescriptive; more story than steps. All authors hope their words will in some way make a difference, reach the right readers, and encourage them to pursue themes that resonate with them. And we hope to stir up some questions and convictions so that readers think about this book's ideas and have conversations about what was read. If that happens we could not be more pleased. And so we end the book with this challenge: Adapt one idea from the epilogue and try it; mash up an idea or two into something that fits your context and try it for a sustained period of time in your ministry, whatever that context might be. Then let us know what happened. Look us up at www.facebook.com/consumingyouth.

ENDNOTES

Introduction

1. Malcolm Gladwell, "The Coolhunt," *The New Yorker*, March 17, 1997. Available at http://www.gladwell.com/1997/1997_03_17_a_cool.htm.

2. Author Susan Linn quoted in Don Aucoin's "All-Consuming Adolescence: Advertisers Are Aiming at an Increasingly Younger Market, and the Kids Are Buying In," *Boston Globe*, December 15, 2004. Available at http://www.boston.com/news/globe/living/articles/2004/12/15/all_consuming_adolescence/.

3. The term "merchants of cool" comes from the *Frontline* (PBS) documentary of the same name with correspondent Douglas Rushkoff. "The Merchants of Cool" originally aired on February 27, 2001, but it can also be viewed on the following website: http://www.pbs.org/wgbh/pages/frontline/shows/cool/.

4. Alissa Quart, *Branded: The Buying and Selling of Teenagers* (New York: Basic Books, 2004), 53.

5. Original broadcast date January 9, 2005.

6. Dori Grinenko Baker and Joyce Ann Mercer, "A Conversation with James Fowler" in *Lives to Offer: Accompanying Youth on Their Vocational Quests* (Cleveland: Pilgrim Press, 2007), 180.

7. The inspiration for this came from a reading of *Media Literacy in Religious Education: Engaging Popular Culture to Enhance Religious Experience*, the 1998 Boston College dissertation of Mary Elizabeth Hess.

8. William Damon, *The Path to Purpose: Helping Our Children Find Their Calling in Life* (New York: Free Press, 2008), 7.

9. See Mark Oestreicher, *Youth Ministry 3.0* (Grand Rapids, Mich.: Zondervan/Youth Specialties, 2008).

10. James E. Côté and Anton L. Allahar, *Generation on Hold: Coming of Age in the Late Twentieth Century* (Toronto: Stoddart, 1994). Also published by New York University Press in 1996. Updated and revised in 2006 as *Critical Youth Studies: A Canadian Focus* (Toronto: Pearson/Prentice Hall).

Chapter 1

1. Frederick Buechner, *Whistling in the Dark: An ABC Theologized* (New York: Harper and Row, 1988), 2.

2. Marie's diaries were published as *I Am the Most Interesting Book of All*. The opening quote and this reference come from the work of Jon Savage in his self-described "prehistory" of the teenager titled *Teenage: The Creation of Youth Culture* (New York: Viking Culture, 2007), 5.

3. At the time of this writing, there were 60,000 hours of material uploaded each week on YouTube. According to producer Ralph Winter, that's the equivalent of 30,000 movies a week, which is an astonishing indicator of the degree to which our culture is making and consuming video. (From a talk presented at the YFC Canada National Staff Conference by Ralph Winter, Edmonton, June 2009.)

4. Joseph Allen, Claudia Worrell Allen, *Escaping the Endless Adolescence: How We Can Help Our Teenagers Grow Up Before They Grow Old* (New York: Ballantine Books, 2009), ix.

5. See chapter 29 in Jon Savage's *Teenage: The Creation of Youth Culture* (New York: Viking Culture, 2007). Thomas Hine also traces the use of the word in *The Rise and Fall of the American Teenager: A New History of the American Adolescent Experience* (New York: Harper Perennial, 1999), 8–9.

6. Thomas Hine, *The Rise and Fall of the American Teenager: A New History of the American Adolescent Experience*, 11.

7. See Chap Clark, "The Changing Face of Adolescence: A Theological View of Human Development," in *Starting Right: Thinking Theologically about Youth Ministry*, eds. Kenda Creasy Dean, Chap Clark, and Dave Rahn (Grand Rapids, Mich.: Zondervan/Youth Specialties, 2001), 45–47.

8. See G. Stanley Hall, *Adolescence: Its Psychology and Its Relations to Physiology, Anthropology, Sociology, Sex, Crime, Religion and Education* (New York: Appleton, 1904).

9. Joseph Kett begins his chapter on the invention of adolescence with this observation in *Rites of Passage: Adolescence in America 1790 to the Present* (New York: Basic Books, 1977), 215. This book is considered to be the classic account of the social construction of adolescence and is well worth reading.

10. See Kett's *Rites of Passage* (pages 221–242) for more about the story on the wide-ranging influence of Hall's work.

11. See Ronald L. Koteskey, "Adolescence as a Cultural Invention," in *Handbook of Youth Ministry*, eds. Donald Ratcliff and James A. Davies (Birmingham, Ala.: Religious Education Press, 1991), 43.

12. See James E. Côté and Anton L. Allahar, *Generation on Hold: Coming of Age in the Late Twentieth Century*. And for a provocative perspective on adolescence, see Robert Epstein, *The Case Against Adolescence: Rediscovering the Adult in Every Teen* (Sanger, Calif.: Quill Driver Books, 2007). Epstein argues that not only is adolescence an unnecessary period of life, but also that people, structures, and systems increasingly treat adolescents more like children than the emerging adults they are (infantilization).

13. Friedrich L. Schweitzer, *The Postmodern Life Cycle: Challenges for Church and Theology* (St. Louis: Chalice Press, 2004), 43.

14. See chapter 1 of *Generation on Hold* for a concise rendering of the "discovery of youth" by Côté and Allahar. See also *the Prologue: Youth and the Invention of Adolescence* to William R. Myers' *Black and White: Styles of Youth Ministry* (New York: Pilgrim Press, 1991) for an interesting personal narrative applied as context to the idea of the invention of adolescence.

15. Hine, *The Rise and Fall of the American Teenager*, 16.

16. See John Demos, *Past, Present, and Personal: The Family and the Life Course in American History* (New York: Oxford University Press, 1986).

17. The idea for these pictures was drawn from the work of Friedrich L. Schweitzer, *The Postmodern Life Cycle*, 6–7. They're intended to be wide-sweeping portraits in order to identify some of the big changes over large periods of time, not to imply a particular normative experience.

18. Kett, *Rites of Passage*, 5–6.

19. Schweitzer, *The Postmodern Life Cycle*, 43.

20. Quentin J. Schultze, Roy M. Anker, James D. Bratt, William D. Romanowski, John W. Worst, and Lambert Zuidervaart, *Dancing in the Dark: Youth, Popular Culture, and the Electronic Media* (Grand Rapids, Mich.: Eerdmans, 1991), 11–12.

21. Don Richter, "Roots and Wings: Practicing Theology with Youth," in *Agenda for Youth Ministry*, eds. Dean Borgman and Christine Cook (London: SPCK Publishing, 1998), 134.

22. See Grace Palladino, *Teenagers: An American History* (New York: Basic Books, 1996). And for a concise and helpful reading to understand the relationship of the adolescent to the workplace, see Harley Atkinson, *Ministry with Youth in Crisis* (Birmingham, Ala.: Religious Education Press, 1997), 150–57.

23. Tony Campolo, *Growing Up in America: A Sociology of Youth Ministry* (Grand Rapids, Mich.: Zondervan, 1989), 27.

24. Brian J. Mahan's book *Forgetting Ourselves on Purpose: Vocation and the Ethics of Ambition* (San Francisco: Jossey-Bass, 2002) is especially helpful in this regard.

25. See Schweitzer, *The Postmodern Life Cycle*, chapter 3.

26. Koteskey, "Adolescence as a Cultural Invention," 52–57.

27. This list is adapted from David F. White, "The Social Construction of Adolescence," in *Awakening Youth Discipleship: Christian Resistance in*

a Consumer Culture, Brian J. Mahan, Michael Warren, and David F. White (Eugene, Ore.: Cascade Books, 2008), 18–19. White's chapter is informative and worth the read, as is the book.

Chapter 2

1. James Côté and Anton Allahar, *Critical Youth Studies: A Canadian Focus* (Toronto: Pearson/Prentice Hall), xiv.

2. Nicole Winfield, "Pope: Ethics Must Guide Quest for Profit," CBS News (July 7, 2009), http://www.cbsnews.com/stories/2009/07/07/world/main5139057.sshtml.

3. G. Stanley Hall, *Adolescence*, 104.

4. There continues to be debate among scholars about the degree to which puberty accounts for teen storm and stress. North American evidence continues to suggest that mood disruptions, risk-taking behavior, and conflicts with parents may be heightened for teenagers relative to other periods of the life course. But scholars continue to disagree with the thesis that adolescence is indelibly linked to stress in all youth. And even Hall himself noted that adolescence was not *only* associated with stress. See, for example, Jeffrey Jensen Arnett, "The Storm and Stress Debate," in *Readings on Adolescence and Emerging Adulthood* (Upper Saddle River, N.J.: Prentice Hall, 2002), 6–17.

5. Margaret Mead, *Coming of Age in Samoa: A Psychological Study of Primitive Youth for Western Civilisation* (New York: Morrow Quill, 1928).

6. This section is highlighting Diana Kendall, *Sociology in Our Times: The Essentials,* 2nd ed. (Belmont, Calif.: Wadsworth Publishing, 1999), 143–144.

7. "Sacred canopies" is a term we've borrowed from Peter L. Berger, as found in his *The Sacred Canopy: Elements of a Sociological Theory of Religion* (Garden City, N.Y.: Doubleday, 1967).

8. This table is adapted from a model by James Côté in *Arrested Adulthood: The Changing Nature of Maturity and Identity* (New York: New York University Press, 2000), 164. It formed the basic structure of the

graph with the added teen trend analysis from Project Teen Canada (25 years) and combined with student research comparing historical understandings of who and what has shaped youth and which institutions were the dominant players in the lives of youth (Sociology of Youth course).

9. Benjamin Barber's *Consumed* (New York: W. W. Norton, 2007) and the research from the Sociology of Youth course historical decade constructs have shaped these generational distinctions and much of the analysis of productive and consumptive capitalism that follows in this section.

10. Naomi Klein, *No Logo: Taking Aim at the Brand Bullies* (Toronto: Alfred A. Knopf, 2000), 5.

11. Much of this next section about the evolution of corporation is taken from *The Corporation,* a film by Mark Achbar, Jennifer Abbott, and Joel Bakan (Mongrel Media, 2005).

12. This section comes from Charles Taylor, *A Secular Age* (London: Harvard University Press, 2007), 473–77.

13. This argument is convincingly made in James Côté and Anton Allahar's *Generation on Hold: Coming of Age in the Late Twentieth Century* (New York: New York University Press, 1996).

14. See, for example, J. J. Arnett, "Emerging Adulthood: A Theory of Development from the Late Teens Through the Twenties," *American Psychologist* 55, no. 5 (2000): 469–80.

15. See Jeremy Rifkin, *The End of Work* (New York: G. P. Putnam's Sons, 1995).

16. See Naomi Klein's *No Logo.*

17. See Naomi Klein's *No Logo* or Todd Gitlin's *Media Unlimited: How the Torrent of Images and Sounds Overwhelms Our Lives* (New York: Henry Holt and Co., 2001).

Chapter 3

1. Mike Mahoney, *All the Right Stuff* (Toronto: National Film Board of Canada, 1997).

2. Tom Beaudoin, *Consuming Faith: Integrating Who We Are with What We Buy* (Lanham, Md.: Sheed and Ward, 2003), 5.

3. See www.quarterlifecrisis.biz.

4. C. Wright Mills, *The Sociological Imagination* (New York: Oxford University Press, 1959).

5. For the insights on the next few pages, we'll draw heavily on James Côté and Anton Allahar's important insights about youth and consumer culture found in their 1996 book *Generation on Hold: Coming of Age in the Late Twentieth Century*, as well as their 2006 update *Critical Youth Studies: A Canadian Focus*.

6. In 1960, 77 percent of women and 65 percent of men had achieved what are considered to be the traditional hallmarks of adulthood: leaving home, graduating school, becoming financially independent, marrying, and having a child. In 2000, those numbers dropped to 46 percent of women and 31 percent of men. See Alexandra Robbins, "Statistics on the Quarterlife Crisis, Twentysomethings, and Young Adults," *QuarterlifeCrisis.biz*, ©2005, http://www.quarterlifecrisis.biz/qc_stats.htm.

7. Quoted in Mahoney, *All the Right Stuff*.

8. See James Côté and Anton Allahar, *Ivory Tower Blues: A University System in Crisis* (Toronto: University of Toronto Press, 2007) for an insightful and relevant analysis of the college and university experience and significant discussion on the themes presented in this section.

9. Reginald W. Bibby, *Canada's Teens: Today, Yesterday, and Tomorrow* (Toronto: Stoddart Publishing, 2001), 134.

10. James Côté and Anton Allahar, *Critical Youth Studies: A Canadian Focus*, 40.

11. Ibid., 41.

12. Ibid.

13. Quoted in Mahoney, *All the Right Stuff*.

14. Allen and Allen, *Escaping the Endless Adolescence*, 143.

15. See Chap Clark, *Hurt: Inside the World of Today's Teenagers* (Grand Rapids, Mich.: Baker, 2004).

16. Patricia Hersch, *A Tribe Apart: A Journey into the Heart of American Adolescence* (New York: Ballantine Books, 1998), 10–30.

17. Edward S. Herman and Noam Chomsky, *Manufacturing Consent: The Political Economy of the Mass Media* (New York: Pantheon, 1988).

18. Peter Wintonick and Mark Achbar, *Manufacturing Consent: Noam Chomsky and the Media* (Zeitgeist Video, 1993).

19. Christian Smith with Melinda Lundquist Denton, *Soul Searching: The Religious and Spiritual Lives of American Teenagers* (New York: Oxford University Press, 2005).

20. Côté and Allahar, *Generation on Hold*, 26.

21. Reginald W. Bibby, *The Emerging Millennials: How Canada's Newest Generation Is Responding to Change and Choice* (Lethbridge: Project Canada Books, 2009).

22. Côté and Allahar, *Generation on Hold*, 27.

23. The PBS documentary "The Merchants of Cool" was the first to detail the midriff identity as well as that of the mook and can be accessed online at: http://www.pbs.org/wgbh/pages/frontline/video/flv/generic.html?s=frol02p70&continuous=1.

Chapter 4

1. David Aikman, *Great Souls: Six Who Changed the Century* (Nashville: Word Publishing, 1998), 202–3.

2. Henri M. Nouwen, *Life of the Beloved: Spiritual Living in a Secular World* (New York: Crossroad Publishing Co., 1992).

3. David F. White, *Practicing Discernment with Youth: A Transformative Youth Ministry Approach* (Cleveland: Pilgrim Press, 2005).

4. Ibid., 58.

5. Ibid., 59.

6. This illustration was inspired by the use of the concept of virus in Douglas Rushkoff, *Media Virus!: Hidden Agendas in Popular Culture* (New York: Ballantine Books, 1994), particularly the explanation of a virus in the introduction.

7. Timothy Shary has written a very accessible book detailing the depiction of teens on film and the development of the "teen movie." See his *Teen Movies: American Youth on Screen* (London: Wallflower Press, 2005), which is a concentrated version of his larger work *Generation Multiplex: The Image of Youth in Contemporary American Cinema* (Austin: University of Texas Press, 2002).

8. See for example the insightful concluding chapter titled "Models of Social Justice for Youth" in James Côté and Anton Allahar's *Critical Youth Studies: A Canadian Focus*, 116–137. This chapter focuses largely on political options to address youth marginalization that perhaps compliment well the focus we put on options for faith communities.

9. James Fowler, *Becoming Adult, Becoming Christian: Adult Development and Christian Faith* (San Francisco: Harper Row, 1984), 95.

10. Parker J. Palmer, *Let Your Life Speak: Listening for the Voice of Vocation* (San Francisco: Jossey-Bass, 2000), 4.

11. Fowler, *Becoming Adult, Becoming Christian*, 95.

12. Parker J. Palmer, *Let Your Life Speak*, 6.

13. Ibid., 5.

14. Aikman, *Great Souls*, 202–203.

15. See Fred P. Edie, *Book, Bath, Table and Time: Christian Worship as Source and Resource for Youth Ministry* (Cleveland: The Pilgrim Press, 2007) 213.

16. See Allen and Allen, *Escaping the Endless Adolescence*, especially part two of the book, where they discuss what it would look like to put adulthood back into adolescence by changing the focus from what it takes to help youth live happily as teenagers to what it takes to help youth move successfully into adulthood.

17. See N.T. Wright, *Simply Christian: Why Christianity Makes Sense* (New York: HarperOne, 2006), especially the final chapter titled "New Creation, Starting Now."

18. Ibid.

19. See Christian Smith with Melinda Lundquist Denton, *Soul Searching: The Religious and Spiritual Lives of American Teenagers*.

20. Christian Smith, "Theorizing Religious Effects Among American Adolescents" *Journal for the Scientific Study of Religion* 42, no. 1 (2003): 17–30.

21. Côté and Allahar, *Critical Youth Studies*, 126.

Chapter 5

1. Joseph Kett, *Rites of Passage: Adolescence in America 1790 to the Present* (New York: Basic Books, 1977), 3.

2. Patricia Hersch, *A Tribe Apart: A Journey into the Heart of American Adolescence* (New York: Ballantine Books, 1998), 364.

3. Nick Hornby, *Slam* (New York: Riverhead Books, 2007), 298–99.

4. See Jean M. Twenge, *Generation Me: Why Today's Young Americans Are More Confident, Assertive, Entitled—and More Miserable Than Ever Before* (New York: Free Press, 2006). Twenge follows up this work with a book that greatly expands on the idea of narcissism which was only really introduced in *Generation Me*. See Jean M. Twenge and W. Keith Campbell, *The Narcissism Epidemic: Living in the Age of Entitlement* (New York: Free Press, 2009).

5. Donald Miller, *A Million Miles in a Thousand Years: What I Learned While Editing My Own Life* (Nashville: Thomas Nelson, 2009), 145. This page reference is from the prepublished galley copy.

6. Michael Warren, "The Imaginations of Youth," in *Awakening Youth Discipleship: Christian Resistance in a Consumer Culture*, Brian J. Mahan, Michael Warren, and David F. White (Eugene, Ore.: Cascade Books, 2008), 44.

7. Rodney Clapp, *Border Crossings: Christian Trespasses on Popular Culture and Public Affairs* (Grand Rapids, Mich.: Brazos, 2000), 127.

8. Mara Einstein, *Brands of Faith: Marketing Religion in a Commercial Age* (New York: Routledge, 2008), 10.

9. Terry O'Reilly and Mike Tennant, *The Age of Persuasion: How Marketing Ate Our Culture* (Toronto: Knopf Canada, 2009), 187. This book is recommended as the place to start for an introduction to the expanding world of marketing from slightly irreverent insiders that examines how marketing (the art of persuasion) shapes our culture.

10. See Kevin Roberts, *Lovemarks: The Future Beyond Brands* (New York: PowerHouse Books, 2005) and the website that, among other things, encourages people to nominate their choice for inclusion as a Lovemark: http://www.lovemarks.com/.

11. See http://www.saatchi.com/.

12. Roberts, *Lovemarks*, chapters 7–10.

13. Clapp, *Border Crossings*, 128.

14. Andrew Root explores this idea further by making the connection between work and love. To have a solid identity one needs to have solid work and solid love. The problem is that work has been replaced by consumption, and love has been replaced by intimacy. Our bodies then become the location of identity: from look, style, to what we hang on our bodies and how we alter them, done in the pursuit of attracting intimacy, resulting in what Root suggests is the death of identity (he calls it a thin identity). See *The Promise of Despair: The Way of the Cross as the Way of the Church* (Nashville: Abingdon Press, 2010), Chapter 4.

15. Alissa Quart, *Branded: The Buying and Selling of Teenagers*, 16.

16. Wendy Murray Zoba, *Generation 2K: What Parents and Others Need to Know About the Millennials* (Downers Grove, Ill.: InterVarsity Press, 1999), 98.

17. Quart, *Branded*, 35.

18. See "The Merchants of Cool," *Frontline* (PBS), original airdate: February 27, 2001. (The entire program can be viewed from the website: http://www.pbs.org/wgbh/pages/frontline/shows/cool/.) This program, including the transcript and longer interviews, is still worth viewing to gain a much greater understanding of cool hunting.

19. Erik H. Erikson, *Identity: Youth and Crisis* (New York: W.W. Norton, 1968), 189.

20. Kenda Creasy Dean, *Practicing Passion: Youth and the Quest for a Passionate Church* (Grand Rapids, Mich.: Eerdmans, 2004), 76.

21. Ibid., 77.

22. Michael Warren, "The Imaginations of Youth," in *Awakening Youth Discipleship: Christian Resistance in a Consumer Culture*, Brian J. Mahan, Michael Warren, and David F. White, 54.

23. The most accessible accounts describing the manner in which adults have pulled away from youth, in contrast to the accepted view that youth are pulling away from adults more than ever before (despite teenagers' desire for a significant adult presence in their lives), are Patricia Hersch, *A Tribe Apart: A Journey into the Heart of American Adolescence*; and part two of Chap Clark, *Hurt: Inside the World of Today's Teenagers*, which talks about the concept of the "world beneath."

24. Dean, *Practicing Passion*, 78.

25. Warren, "The Imaginations of Youth," 56–57. For those who lead or teach youth work courses, Warren suggests it's "time to shift the canonical or 'must readings'" lists in an attempt to broaden, complement, or even offer alternatives to Erikson. He recommends beginning with Charles Taylor, *Sources of the Self: The Making of the Modern Identity* (Cambridge, Mass.: Harvard University Press, 1989).

26. C. S. Lewis, *The Magician's Nephew* (New York: Collier Books, 1970), 125. This was sparked by a similar usage of this passage by Steven Garber in *The Fabric of Faithfulness: Weaving Together Belief and Behavior During the University Years* (Downers Grove, Ill.: InterVarsity Press, 1996).

27. Einstein, *Brands of Faith*, xi.

Chapter 6

1. This quote is attributed to Dr. Jay Kesler, the former president of Youth for Christ International and later Taylor University. It was originally cited in a May 1985 *Group Magazine* article by Thom Shultz. Mark Senter used the quote to open his 1989 doctoral dissertation on the history and impact of youth ministry, and he made the observation that if Kesler were pressed to explain what he meant by the statement, it's very likely that he'd admit he'd overstated his case a bit. For those wanting a substantive reading of the history of youth ministry, see Mark Senter, *The Youth for Christ Movement as an Educational Agency and Its Impact upon Protestant Churches: 1931–1979* (Ann Arbor, Mich.: University Microfilms International, 1990).

2. Mark Oestreicher, *Youth Ministry 3.0* (Grand Rapids, Mich.: Zondervan/Youth Specialties, 2008), 45.

3. Posted by Professor Darwin Glassford on the "Youth Ministry 3.0" Facebook discussion group, January 28, 2009.

4. For more information on the Akron Plan architectural style, you can take a look at a collection of posted photos on Flickr at http://www.flickr.com/photos/millinerd/sets/72157594456660327/ or read a Web page written by Brother Christopher Stephen Jenks, an architectural historian and preservationist, at http://www.sacredplaces.org/PSP-InfoClearingHouse/articles/American%20Religious%20Buildings.htm.

5. Robert W. Lynn and Elliott Wright, *The Big Little School: Sunday Child of American Protestantism* (San Francisco: Harper and Row, 1971), 83.

6. The extent and range of events, places, and personalities associated with a history of youth ministry is well beyond the size and scope of

this and the next chapter. Our aim is to relate just enough of the youth ministry story to begin asking how the rise of a culturally constructed and accepted version of adolescence and the concurrent growth of a consumer market economy have impacted both the shape of youth ministry and the response of the church to adolescence. The story told here has been shaped in large measure by Mark Senter's *The Coming Revolution in Youth Ministry: And Its Radical Impact on the Church* (Wheaton, Ill.: Victor Books, 1992), and as we finish up this work, that book has just been published in a substantially revised and enlarged edition titled, *When God Shows Up: A History of Protestant Youth Ministry in America* (Grand Rapids, Mich.: Baker Academic, 2010); see also *The Youth for Christ Movement as an Educational Agency and Its Impact on Protestant Churches: 1931–1979* (Ann Arbor, Mich.: University Microfilms International, 1990) by Senter; Dean Borgman, "A History of American Youth Ministry," in *The Complete Book of Youth Ministry*, eds. Warren S. Benson and Mark H. Senter III (Chicago: Moody Press, 1987); Mark W. Cannister, "Youth Ministry's Historical Context: The Education and Evangelism of Young People," in *Starting Right: Thinking Theologically about Youth Ministry*, eds. Kenda Creasy Dean, Chap Clark, and Dave Rahn (Grand Rapids, Mich.: Zondervan/Youth Specialties, 2001) 77–90; Jon Pahl, *Youth Ministry in Modern America: 1930 to the Present* (Peabody, Mass.: Hendrickson Publishers, 2000); and Bruce Shelley, "The Rise of Evangelical Youth Movements," *Fides et Historia: Volume 18* (1986): 47–63. From a British perspective, Pete Ward's, *Growing Up Evangelical: Youthwork and the Making of a Subculture* (London: SPCK, 1996) has been helpful and influential. And to obtain additional perspective of the people and personalities connected to a history of youth ministry, we referred to the two articles by Mark Cannister, "Youth Ministry Pioneers of the 20th Century, Part I and Part II," *Christian Education*, 3rd series, 1 no. 1 (2003): 66–72 and 176–188.

7. Mark W. Cannister, "Youth Ministry's Historical Context: The Education and Evangelism of Young People," in *Starting Right: Thinking Theologically about Youth Ministry*, 77.

8. Lynn and Wright, *The Big Little School*, 4.

9. Ibid., 5.

10. YMCA, "History of the YMCA Movement," *YMCA*, http://www
.ymca.net/about_the_ymca/history_of_the_ymca.html; and World
YWCA, "Our History," *World YWCA*, http://www.worldywca.org/en/
About-us/Our-History.

11. David F. White "The Social Construction of Adolescence" in *Awakening Youth Discipleship: Christian Resistance in a Consumer Culture*, Brian
J. Mahan, Michael Warren, David F. White (Eugene, Ore.: Cascade
Books, 2008), 9.

12. Mark Cannister, "Back to the Future: A Historical Perspective,"
Christian Education Journal, n.s., 3 no. 2 (1999): 22.

13. See Sara Little, "Youth Ministry: Historical Reflections Near the
End of the Twentieth Century," in *At-Risk Youth, At-Risk Church: What
Jesus Christ and American Teenagers Are Saying to the Mainline Church*,
The Institute for Youth Ministry, 1997 Princeton Lectures on Youth,
Church, and Culture (Princeton, NJ: Princeton Theological Seminary,
1998), 11–23. Available at http://www.ptsem.edu/iym/lectures/1997/
index.php. See also Kenda Creasy Dean in *Practicing Passion*, 147–149
(especially note 11) for additional discussion on this point.

14. Dean Borgman, "A History of American Youth Ministry," in *The
Complete Book of Youth Ministry*, eds. Warren S. Benson and Mark H.
Senter III (Chicago: Moody Press, 1987), 71. See also the helpful
youth ministry timeline prepared by Mark Cannister in "Youth Ministry's Historical Context: The Education and Evangelism of Young
People," in *Starting Right: Thinking Theologically about Youth Ministry*.

15. See Mark Cannister, "Youth Ministry Pioneers of the 20th Century,
Part I," *Christian Education Journal*, 3rd series, 1 no. 1 (2003); 68-69;
and Mark Senter, *The Coming Revolution in Youth Ministry: And Its Radical
Impact on the Church* (Wheaton, Ill.: Victor Books, 1992).

16. Cannister, "Youth Ministry Pioneers of the 20th Century, Part I,"
Christian Education Journal, 3rd series, 1 no. 1 (2003): 69.

17. Jon Savage, *Teenage: The Creation of Youth Culture* (New York:
Viking Culture, 2007), 318–320.

18. Senter, *The Youth for Christ Movement*, 141.

19. See chapter 7 of Joseph Kett, *Rites of Passage*.

Chapter 7

1. Jon Savage, *Teenage: The Creation of Youth Culture*, 465.

2. Ibid.

3. Mark Senter, *The Coming Revolution in Youth Ministry: And Its Radical Impact on the Church*, 117. As with the previous chapter, both this book and those works cited in chapter 6 have been influential for the recounting of this story.

4. To reiterate, the extent and range of places, events, and personalities associated with a history of youth ministry is well beyond the intent of this chapter. Our aim is to relate just enough of the story that allows us to begin asking how the rise of a culturally invented adolescence and the concurrent growth of consumer culture have impacted the shape of youth ministry and the response of the church to adolescence.

5. Dean Borgman, "A History of American Youth Ministry," in *The Complete Book of Youth Ministry*, 68.

6. See Emile Cailliet, *Young Life* (New York: Harper and Row, 1963), and Char Meredith, *It's a Sin to Bore a Kid: The Story of Young Life* (Waco, Texas: Word Books, 1978).

7. See Meredith, *It's a Sin to Bore a Kid*, 45–46.

8. The founders of Youth Specialties (Wayne Rice and Mike Yaconelli) were staff members with YFC and among the influential shapers in the development of this club strategy. In *Youth Ministry 3.0* (Grand Rapids, Mich.: Zondervan/Youth Specialties, 2008), Mark Oestreicher makes reference to a humorous and interesting bit of their story related to the sale of their first resources, as does Mark Senter in *The Coming Revolution*.

9. Conservative Protestant churches, broadly defined evangelical churches, and mainline congregations and parishes all were hiring youth pastors.

10. See Andrew Root, *Revisiting Relational Youth Ministry: From a Strategy of Influence to a Theology of Incarnation* (Downers Grove, Ill.: InterVarsity Press, 2007), for a challenging blend of missional and theological thinking on the nature of relationships in ministry.

11. Helpful in this regard is Kenda Creasy Dean's "Theological Rocks—First Things First" and "Fessing Up: Owning Our Theological Commitments," in *Starting Right: Thinking Theologically about Youth Ministry*, 15–39. Also Dean Borgman, *When Kumbaya Is Not Enough: A Practical Theology for Youth Ministry* (Peabody, Mass.: Hendrickson Publishers, 1997). A much broader examination is found in Pete Ward's *Participation and Mediation: A Practical Theology for the Liquid Church* (London: SCM Press, 2008). And for an accessible and practical application, see Chap Clark and Kara Powell, *Deep Ministry in a Shallow World: Not-So-Secret Findings about Youth Ministry* (Grand Rapids, Mich.: Zondervan/Youth Specialties, 2006).

12. Senter, *The Coming Revolution*, 147–148.

13. Mike King, *Presence-Centered Youth Ministry: Guiding Students into Spiritual Formation* (Downers Grove, Ill.: InterVarsity Press, 2006), 32.

14. Ibid., 33.

15. Don Richter, "Roots and Wings: Practicing Theology with Youth," in *Agenda for Youth Ministry*, eds. Dean Borgman and Christine Cook (London: SPCK, 1998), 136–140.

16. Ibid., 137.

17. See Pete Ward, *Growing Up Evangelical: Youthwork and the Making of a Subculture* (London: SPCK, 1996), especially part three: "Safety and the Subculture." And for those wanting a very compelling and generous outsider's look at the alternative youth Christian subculture, see Andrew Beaujon, *Body Piercing Saved My Life: Inside the Phenomenon of Christian Rock* (Cambridge, Mass.: Da Capo Press, 2006).

18. Don Richter, "Roots and Wings," 137.

19. Ibid., 139.

20. Alan Hirsch, *The Forgotten Ways: Reactivating the Missional Church*

(Grand Rapids, Mich.: Brazos Press, 2001), 107.

21. See Kenda Creasy Dean, *Practicing Passion: Youth and the Quest for a Passionate Church*.

Chapter 8

1. Frederick Buechner, *Wishful Thinking: A Seeker's ABC* (New York: Harper and Row, 1993), 118–119.

2. Annie Dillard, *Teaching a Stone to Talk: Expeditions and Encounters* (New York: Harper and Row, 1982), 69–70.

3. The title of this chapter, "Lives to Offer," significantly stuck with us from the book by the same name by Dori Grinenko Baker and Joyce Ann Mercer, *Lives to Offer: Accompanying Youth on Their Vocational Quests* (Cleveland: Pilgrim Press, 2007).

4. Michael D. Wiese, *The Samuel Project: A Study of Pastoral Development in the Church* (Anderson, Ind.: General Conference and Mennonite Church in the United States and Canada, 1999), 29.

5. John Neufeld, former director of the Ministry Quest project and now a senior pastor, has written a booklet called "Finding Leaders for Tomorrow's Churches" to assist congregations with the discernment of leaders. It can be downloaded as a PDF from http://www.mbconf.ca/home/products_and_services/resources/leadership_development/finding_leaders_for_tomorrows_churches/.

6. See Arnold van Gennep, *The Rites of Passage* (Chicago: University of Chicago Press, 1961) and Victor Turner, *The Ritual Process: Structure and Anti-Structure* (New York: Cornell University Press, 1969).

7. See Allen and Allen, *Escaping the Endless Adolescence*, 160–62.

Chapter 9

1. William Damon, *The Path to Purpose: Helping Our Children Find Their Calling in Life* (New York: Free Press, 2008), 33.

2. Dori Grinenko Baker and Joyce Ann Mercer, *Lives to Offer: Accompanying Youth on Their Vocational Quests*, 8. Note also that part of this chapter title ("Stories Worth Living") comes from chapter 5 of their book.

3. In *Lives to Offer*, Dori Grinenko Baker and Joyce Ann Mercer suggest that vocation is the central theme of youth ministry.

4. Robert Aubrey and Paul Cohen, *Working Wisdom: Timeless Skills and Vanguard Strategies for Learning Organizations* (San Francisco: Jossey-Bass, 1995), 39.

5. Deborah van Deusen Hunsinger, "Vocation: A Joyous Task" in *Compass Points: Navigating Vocation—2002 Princeton Lectures on Youth, Church, and Culture* (Princeton, N.J.: Princeton Theological Seminary, 2002), 15.

6. Sharon Daloz Parks, *Big Questions, Worthy Dreams: Mentoring Young Adults in Their Search for Meaning, Purpose, and Faith* (San Francisco: Jossey-Bass, 2000). A very helpful way to envision the mentoring task is provided by Laurent A. Daloz in his book *Mentor* (San Francisco: Jossey-Bass, Second Edition, 1999). Though the book is geared to the journey of adult learners, his discussion of the importance and application of challenge and support—and the practices that enhance them—is easily adaptable in youth work and does provide a workable and accessible approach for mentoring youth.

7. See also the work of Jeffrey Jensen Arnett in this regard, especially his book *Emerging Adulthood: The Winding Road from the Late Teens through the Twenties* (New York: Oxford University Press, 2004). This book, when read together with Parks', provides youth workers with the necessary vision to understand how the extension of adolescence has dramatically altered the road to adulthood.

Epilogue

1. William Willimon, "Imitating Christ in a Postmodern World: Making Young Disciples Today" in *Growing Up Postmodern: Imitating Christ in the Age of "Whatever"—1998 Princeton Lectures on Youth, Church, and Culture* (Princeton, N.J.: Princeton Theological Seminary, 1999), 100.

2. Laurent A. Parks Daloz, Cheryl H. Keen, James P. Keen, Sharon Daloz Parks, *Common Fire: Lives of Commitment in a Complex World* (Boston: Beacon Press, 1996), 229.

3. This story is from Willimon, "Imitating Christ in a Postmodern World: Making Young Disciples Today" in *Growing Up Postmodern*, 100–101.

4. Thomas Hine, *The Rise and Fall of the American Teenager: A New History of the American Adolescent Experience*, 296–304.

5. Ibid., 304.

6. See, for example, "Youth No Longer Defined by Age; Consumers Stay 'Younger' Longer," *Marketing VOX: The Voice of Online Marketing*, posted October 27, 2008, at http://www.marketingvox.com/youth-no-longer-defined-by-age-consumers-stay-younger-longer-041658/?camp=rssfeed&src=mv&type=textlink. It contains results from the "Golden Age of Youth" study. Among other things, this article reports that (a) the traditional demographic definition of "youth" is no longer applicable in today's society, (b) marketers should target consumers based upon their engagement and participation in youth culture, rather than by chronological age, and (c) as people worldwide delay the onset of adult responsibilities and stay emotionally and physically younger for longer, it's becoming more acceptable for older people to participate in youthful pursuits. See also chapter 1 of Quentin J. Schultze, Roy M. Anker, James D. Bratt, William D. Romanowski, John W. Worst, and Lambert Zuidervaart, *Dancing in the Dark: Youth, Popular Culture, and the Electronic Media* (Grand Rapids, Mich.: Eerdmans, 1991), 5–6.

7. Friedrich L. Schweitzer, *The Postmodern Life Cycle: Challenges for Church and Theology* (St. Louis: Chalice Press, 2004), 55. See also the section from pages 55 through 63.

8. The interview is about his six-year study following students from high school into their first year after graduation, titled *The First Year Out: Understanding American Teens after High School* (Chicago University Press, 2007). The interview, titled "Life After High School: The First Year," can be found on the Center for Parent/Youth Understanding website at http://www.cpyu.org/Page.aspx?id=387650. For those look-

ing for a little more, there is a helpful podcast with Clydesdale through Princeton's Institute for Youth Ministry at http://www3.pptsem.edu/ offices/coned/iym/Podcast/. And this February 2007 article titled "Abandoned, Pursued, or Safely Stowed?" explores the notion of the "lockbox" theory (available at http://religion.ssrc.org/reforum/Clydesdale.pdf). The Fuller Youth Institute has also explored Clydesdale's work. See Meredith Miller, "The Lockbox Theory's Implications for Your Students," *Fuller Youth Institute*, October 7, 2008, http://fulleryouthinstitute.org/2008/10/the-lockbox-theory%E2%80%99s-implications-for-your-students/.

9. Clydesdale interview with Melleby.

10. Ibid.

11. Willimon, "Imitating Christ in a Postmodern World: Making Young Disciples Today," 101.

12. See Katherine Turpin, *Branded: Adolescents Converting from Consumer Faith* (Cleveland: The Pilgrim Press, 2006). Turpin addresses the problem of consumer culture from the perspective of "ongoing conversion" experienced in educational structures like that of a small group to shake loose the grip that consumerism has on teenagers.

13. This story is from Joyce Ann Mercer, "Are We Going on Vocation Now? Ministry with Youth as a Lifelong Vocation" in *Compass Points: Navigating Vocation'—2002 Princeton Lectures on Youth, Church, and Culture* (Princeton, N.J.: Princeton Theological Seminary, 2002), 52–53.

14. Baker uses *The Message* to unpack the Sermon on the Mount, http://www.ivcf.ca/ivcf/myweb.php?hls=10125.

15. Tom Sine, *The New Conspirators: Creating the Future One Mustard Seed at a Time* (Downers Grove, Ill.: InterVarsity Press, 2008), 297. A related and interesting new project being developed by Scott Moore and Paul Bartley (also of Toronto Youth Unlimited in partnership with World Vision Canada) is *Blueprints*. The project goal is for youth to create and implement a blueprint that launches a business concept or idea or helps youth pursue a chosen profession. It's being developed in the Jane-Finch community of Toronto (one of the city's most ethnically diverse and impoverished communities) and addresses the need its young

people have for: (a) receiving practical and applicable education for all areas of life, (b) breaking down negative stereotyping, and (c) forming positive relationships with peers and adults.

16. Ibid., 297.

17. Ibid., 297–98.

18. Joseph Kett, *Rites of Passage: Adolescence in America 1790 to the Present* (New York: Basic Books, 1977), 6.

19. Schultze, et al., *Dancing in the Dark*, 9.

20. Eugene Peterson, *Leap Over a Wall: Earthly Spirituality for Everyday Christians* (San Francisco: HarperSanFrancisco, 1997), 54.

21. William Damon, *The Path to Purpose: Helping our Children Find Their Calling in Life* (New York: Free Press, 2008), 96.

22. Mark Yaconelli, *Contemplative Youth Ministry: Practicing the Presence of Jesus* (Grand Rapids, Mich.: Zondervan/Youth Specialties, 2006), 172–76.

23. Ibid., 175.

24. Mike Yaconelli, *Getting Fired for the Glory of God: Collected Words of Mike Yaconelli for Youth Workers* (Grand Rapids, Mich.: Zondervan/ Youth Specialties, 2008), 57.

Share Your Thoughts

With the Author: Your comments will be forwarded to the author when you send them to *zauthor@zondervan.com*.

With Zondervan: Submit your review of this book by writing to *zreview@zondervan.com*.

Free Online Resources at
www.zondervan.com

Zondervan AuthorTracker: Be notified whenever your favorite authors publish new books, go on tour, or post an update about what's happening in their lives at www.zondervan.com/authortracker.

Daily Bible Verses and Devotions: Enrich your life with daily Bible verses or devotions that help you start every morning focused on God. Visit www.zondervan.com/newsletters.

Free Email Publications: Sign up for newsletters on Christian living, academic resources, church ministry, fiction, children's resources, and more. Visit www.zondervan.com/newsletters.

Zondervan Bible Search: Find and compare Bible passages in a variety of translations at www.zondervanbiblesearch.com.

Other Benefits: Register yourself to receive online benefits like coupons and special offers, or to participate in research.

ZONDERVAN®

ZONDERVAN.com/
AUTHORTRACKER
follow your favorite authors